SOUNDS OF LANGUAGE

readers

This book is dedicated to my friend
PAUL A. WITTY
who first acquainted me
with the naturality of reading

SOUNDS
OF A YOUNG
HUNTER

BY BILL MARTIN JR.
IN COLLABOR- PEGGY BROGAN
ATION WITH

Holt, Rinehart and Winston, Inc., New York, Toronto, London, Sydney

Acknowledgments

The Author and Holt, Rinehart and Winston, Inc., thank the following authors, publishers, agents and parties whose help and permissions to reprint materials have made this book possible. If any errors in acknowledgments have occurred, the errors were inadvertent and will be corrected in subsequent editions as they are realized.

Addison-Wesley, Inc., Publisher, for "The Ant, the Lamb, the Cricket and the Mouse," from *The Boy Who Could Do Anything and Other Mexican Folk Tales,* by Anita Brenner. Copyright 1942 by Anita Brenner. Permission granted by the publisher, Addison-Wesley, Inc.

The American Artists' Group for the illustrations on pages 206-207 by Jerome Snyder.

Atheneum Publishers, for "Beware, or Be Yourself," from *It Doesn't Always Have to Rhyme,* by Eve Merriam. Copyright © 1964 by Eve Merriam. Used by permission.

The Bliss Carman Trust, for "A Vagabond Song," by Bliss Carman, from *Bliss Carman's Poems,* published by Dodd, Mead & Company, Inc. Copyright 1929 by Bliss Carman. Reprinted by special permission of the Bliss Carman Trust, The University of New Brunswick, Canada.

Bobbs-Merrill Company, Inc., for the lines from "At Ninety in the Shade," "It," and "A Song for Singing," from *The Complete Poetical Works of James Whitcomb Riley,* published in 1937 by Bobbs-Merrill Company, Inc. Copyright 1937 by Bobbs-Merrill Company, Inc. and Mary Riley Payne, Elizabeth Eitel Miesse, and Edmund H. Eitel. Reprinted by permission.

Michael Brent Publications, Inc., Port Chester, New York, for "Legend of the Twelve Moons," excerpts from the historical cantata, *Legend of the Twelve Moons,* narration written by Ruth Roberts, and all songs written by Ruth Roberts except one in collaboration with William Katz. The entire cantata copyright © 1969 and 1970 by Michael Brent Publications, Inc., through which source the entire cantata is available. All rights reserved.

Nick Calabrese, for his painting, "Scandinavian Winter Night," on page 371.

Curtis Publishing Company, for "Gift with the Wrappings Off," by Mary Elizabeth Counselman, from *The Saturday Evening Post.* Copyright 1939 by The Curtis Publishing Company. Reprinted by permission.

J. M. Dent and Songs, Ltd. for "Johnnie Crack and Flossie Snail," from *Under Milk Wood,* by Dylan Thomas. Reprinted by permission of J. M. Dent and Sons, Ltd.

The Dial Press, Inc., for "Song of the Pop-Bottlers," from *A Bowl of Bishop,* by Morris Bishop. Copyright © 1954 by Morris Bishop. Reprinted by permission of the Publisher.

Dodd, Mead & Company, Inc., for "Here Is This Night," from *Silver Saturday,* by Nancy Byrd Turner. Copyright 1937 by Dodd, Mead & Company. Used by permission.

Doubleday & Company, Inc., Publishers, for "doing well," from ARCHY DOES HIS PART by Don Marquis. Copyright 1920 by Sun Printing and Publishing Association. Reprinted by permission of Doubleday & Company, Inc.

United Feature Syndicate, Inc., for the illustration for "Suppertime," from PEANUTS CARTOONS, and used by permission of United Feature Syndicate, Inc., © 1961, 1962, 1963.

To HIRO, for the photos on pages 344 and 366. Used with his permission.

The Viking Press for "The Cornfield," from UNDER THE TREE, by Elizabeth Madox Roberts. Copyright 1922 by B. W. Huebsch, Inc. Renewed 1950 by Ivor S. Roberts. Reprinted by permission of The Viking Press, Inc. All rights reserved.

The Viking Press, Inc., for "Cow," from the chapter "Barn News," from MISS HICKORY, by Carolyn Sherwin Bailey, with lithographs by Ruth Gannett. Copyright 1946 by Carolyn Sherwin Bailey. Reprinted by permission of The Viking Press, Inc.

S. D. Warren Company, for the painting, "Parade," by Allan Mardon, on page 360. Used with their courtesy.

The World's Work Ltd., Surrey, England, for "If Once You Have Slept on an Island," a poem taken from TAXIS AND TOADSTOOLS, by Rachel Field. Reprinted by permission of the British publishers, The World's Work Ltd.

The World's Work Ltd., Surrey, England, for "Meeting," a poem taken from TAXIS AND TOADSTOOLS, by Rachel Field, published in Great Britain by the World's Work Ltd.

Williamson Music, Inc., New York, for "THE SOUND OF MUSIC," lyrics from the musical composition, THE SOUND OF MUSIC. Copyright © 1959 by Richard Rodgers and Oscar Hammerstein II. Reprinted by permission of Williamson Music, Inc., New York.

Williamson Music, Inc., New York, and Williamson Music Ltd., London, for "YOU'LL NEVER WALK ALONE," lines from the musical composition CAROUSEL. Copyright 1945 by Richard Rodgers and Oscar Hammerstein II. Used by permission of the publishers, Williamson Music, Inc., New York and Williamson Music Ltd., London.

Acknowledgement is made to Judy Kopecky, Paul Waldman, Allen Moss and Lex Caiola who prepared the front matter.

Acknowledgment is also made to Betty Jean Martin for permission to use the character, Noodles the Ghost, in this edition of *Sounds of a Young Hunter.*

And no acknowledgment list would be complete without special thanks and appreciation to Lydia Vita, Mel Rohr and Victor Hernandez for their skilled preparation of this book for delivery to the printer.

TABLE OF CONTENTS
PART I
FIGURING OUT HOW READING WORKS

PART II

RESPONDING TO READING

PART I

Bill: Hello, boys and girls.
This is your friend, Bill Martin.

Noodles: Oodeley, oodeley.

Bill: And Noodles is here.
Noodles where are you?
I can't see you.

Noodles: That's because I'm a ghost.

Bill: Where are you, Noodles?

Noodles: I'm hiding.

Bill: Noodles, now stop this foolishness.
These boys and girls
are waiting to meet you.

Noodles: I already did meet them.

Bill: Then come say hello to your friends.

Noodles: Tell me one thing.
Are you going to talk a lot again
and go on and on
until I'm so tired I can't stand it?

Bill: Oh, Noodles, I never talk that much.

Noodles: You don't think so because
you don't have to listen to you, Bill Martin.

Bill: Then I promise, I'll not talk too much.

Noodles: All right, then. Here I come . . .

APPEAR
APPEAR
APPEAR
APPEAR
APPEAR
APPEAR

Here I am.
Hello, boys and girls.
Hello, Bill Martin.

Bill: Good morning, Noodles.
Isn't it exciting to be starting a new book?

Noodles: Yes, and this is one of my favorite books
because it's got a lot of short stories
in it and I like short stories.

Bill: *Sounds of a Young Hunter.*

Noodles: Bill, you're talking too much.

Bill: Am I, boys and girls?

Noodles: They can't answer you.

Bill: Why not?

Noodles: Because I asked them not to but
you're talking too much.

Bill: Oh, Noodles.

Noodles: I think I'll go now.

Bill:	But could I ask you one question, Noodles? Just one.
Noodles:	Well, maybe, just one.
Bill:	Will you tell the boys and girls what this little rendezvous is all about?
Noodles:	This little what?
Bill:	This little meeting we're having.
Noodles:	I don't know. I suppose because it's school.
Bill:	No, Noodles, it's becau ...
Noodles:	Goodbye, Bill. Goodbye.
Bill:	Please help me, Noodles. Please.
Noodles:	Pretty please with sugar on it?
Bill:	Yes, pretty please with sugar on it.
Noodles:	All right, Bill Martin. Boys and girls, we're here right now to invite you to *Sounds of a Young Hunter,* where everything squeaks and haunts and blows and blusters and laughs and sings and dances and coos and prods and pries and pushes and pulls ... and talks too much.
Bill:	This book will help you know what you already know

about reading
but perhaps didn't know
that you knew.

Noodles: Say, that really is my big problem.
I know everything
but just can't remember it.

Bill: *Sounds of a Young Hunter*
is divided into two parts.
Part I which we've just begun
is "Figuring Out How Reading Works."
Part II is "Responding to What You Read."

Noodles: Hey, Bill Martin,
that sounds pretty dull.
I think I'll go now.
But before I go
just so you won't sit here
and talk talk talk, Bill Martin,
I'm going to turn you into a blot.

Bill: Oh, no, Noodles. Not right now.

Noodles: Hokus pokus diddeley dokus . . .
Bill Martin you're changing into a blot.

Bill: Oh, no, No - o - o - o - - - - -

Noodles: There! Bill Martin is now a blot!
We've got to take care of
one another, right, boys and girls?
So goodbye.
Oodeley, oodeley.

the
Cry
of the
Wild Goose

Tonight I heard the wild goose cry
Wingin' north in the lonely sky,
Tried to sleep but it warn't no use,
'Cause I am a brother to the old wild goose.

My heart knows what the wild goose knows
and I must go where the wild goose goes,
Wild goose, brother goose, which is best,
A wand'rin' foot or a heart at rest?
My heart knows what the wild goose knows
and I must go where the wild goose goes,
Wild goose, brother goose, which is best,
A wand'rin' foot or a heart at rest?

A SONG BY TERRY GILKYSON, ART BY TED RAND

The Gray Marauder

A story by Paul Brown,
pictures by Michael Lowenbein

WAR PAINT was a wild range colt. He roamed the Western prairies where once the Crow, Cheyenne, Kiowa and Comanche Indians had fought on the warpath. One day he followed an older colt named Nosey on an exploring expedition. The two wandered off from the band, but they didn't go very far.

This brief episode is taken from a book, War Paint: An Indian Pony, by Paul Brown. If you like it and want to read the entire book, ask for it at your library or bookstore. The pictures here by Michael Lowenbein do not appear in the book. They were done especially for this excerpt.

War Paint wanted to turn back when his mother nickered to him, but Nosey said, "Oh, come on, let's see what's in this gully!"

The two explorers had gone just a little bit farther when suddenly a stone rattled down a bank.

The colts whirled about.
There was a great gray prairie wolf!
Instantly the colts started toward the herd,
but the wolf cut off their retreat.
The startled youngsters bolted off on a new tack
seeking escape in another direction,
and Nosey found a way out and scooted up a bank to safety.
War Paint followed,
but the wolf was there before him.
Scared out of his wits,
the spotted colt doubled back.
He dodged away, but the killer
was upon him
and leaped in to sever the hamstring[1]
in one of the little fellow's hind legs.
War Paint lashed out with his heels.
He did little damage, but he made
the powerful jaws miss their mark.
Once again he fled, this time squealing
with pain from a bloody gash in his rump.
Over the rocks he clattered,
but in a second he was cornered.
The little colt was wild eyed with fear,
for straight at him came the great gray wolf.
War Paint was at his mercy.
In a flash it would be all over.

[1] tendon behind and above the
hock—wolves try to cripple
their victims in this way

23

Intent upon his tender victim, the wolf had not heard the thudding of feet on the rim of the ravine. A bay[2] thunderbolt was coming down the rocky hillside. Ears laid back, eyes flashing, and teeth bare, War Paint's mother suddenly hurtled upon the scene. The wolf seemed to stop his last leap in midair, but he was too late. With a lightning-fast thrust of her head, the mare sank her teeth deep in the wolf's skin, and with a great toss of her head, she flung him end over end into some chaparral.[3] Murder was in her heart as she flew after her victim, but he scrambled up and avoided her flailing forefeet. Away he scurried with his tail between his legs, and just in time, too, for into the gully galloped several young stallions that had raced to the defense.

[2] a reddish-brown colored horse with black mane and tail

[3] dense thicket of small trees or shrubs

The mare soon gave up the vain pursuit and returned to inspect her trembling colt. "After this, you come the first time you are called," she said, and with a rough nudge of her nose, she hustled him back to the band.

A story by Tom Sankey

FLETCHER AND CRACKER

Cracker was down
at Hiram Handy's store one day
when he spotted a box of old junk
that Hiram was throwing out.

"Can I take this box of junk?"
says Cracker.

"Sure," says Hiram,
"but I'll tell you right now
that stuff is worthless.
Everything in it is torn or broken."

"Oh, that's all right, Hiram,"
says Cracker.
"I'll find a use for it."

And he closed the lid on the box,
hefted it to his shoulder
and started on down the road
to Fletcher's house.

When he got to Fletcher's farm,
he set the box down
next to the front gate
and began to sigh and groan.
Fletcher came out of his house
to see what was the matter.

"Hello, there, Cracker,"
says Fletcher.
"What's the matter?"

"Hello, Fletcher," says Cracker.
"My surprise package
is too heavy for me,
that's what's the matter."

"Surprise package?" says Fletcher.
"What's in it, Cracker?"

"Don't know," says Cracker.
"That's why it's called
a surprise package."

"Why don'tcha open it up?"
says Fletcher.

"I was waiting to get it home,"
says Cracker,
"but it don't look
like I'm going to make it.
It's probably full of a lot of things
I don't need.
Who needs surprises, anyway?"

"How much do you want
for the box?" says Fletcher.

"This old thing?" says Cracker.
"Oh, you don't want this old thing."

"Yes I do, yes I do," says Fletcher.
"How much?"

"Oh, not much," says Cracker.
"Let's say a dollar
  for this worthless box
  full of wonderful surprises."

"I'll take it!" says Fletcher,
  fishing a dollar out of his pocket.

Fletcher tore open the box.
The first thing he pulled out
was an old boot with the sole missing.

"Oh, shucks!" says Fletcher,
  and he tossed the boot
  over his shoulder
  and reached into the box again.

"Oh, rats!" says Fletcher,
  as he hauled out a jacket
  with one sleeve missing.
  This, too, he flung over his shoulder.

"Durnit," says Fletcher,
  as he dumped the remaining contents
  of the box on the lawn.
"None of this stuff is any good.
  Look here, a bucket
  with a hole in the bottom,
  a hoe with the handle broken off
  and a wrecked umbrella!
  All this junk!"

"Oh, that so?" says Cracker.
"Since you're so disappointed,
  I'll buy that stuff back from you.
  Here's your dollar."

Fletcher grabbed the dollar
  out of Cracker's hand.
"I don't mean to be a bad sport,"
  he says, "but at least now
  you don't have to haul
  that junk home."

"Oh, that's all right, Fletcher,"
  says Cracker,
"I'll find a use for it."

"This stuff?" says Fletcher.
"How can you use this stuff?"

"Oh," says Cracker,
"it's easy to find a use
  for most anything
  if you want to."

He picked up the boot.
"Now this boot here.
  Not much good as a boot.
  Know what I'm going to do with it?"

"No," says Fletcher.
"You gonna hop around on one foot?"

"Umbrella stand," says Cracker.

"Huh!" says Fletcher.
"The sole's missing.
  It's got a hole in the bottom."

"To let the rain water drain out,"
  says Cracker.

"Say!" says Fletcher.
"I could use that!
  How much
  you want for it, Cracker?"

"Ten cents," says Cracker.

"Sold!" says Fletcher.

"How about that jacket, now?
  Whatcha gonna do with that?"

"A jacket with one sleeve missing
  is nothing," says Cracker.
"But a jacket
  with two sleeves missing
  ...is a vest."

29

cough, cough, cough, cough, cough, cough, cough,

He picked up the jacket
and tore the other sleeve off.

"That looks like it might fit me,"
says Fletcher.

"Twenty cents," says Cracker.

"Sold!" says Fletcher.

Cracker picked up the bucket.
"Well, well," he says.
"You know,
I wouldn't call this a bucket—
I'd call it a radish waterer."

"It's a bucket with a hole in it,
no matter what you call it,"
says Fletcher.

"That's true, that's true,"
says Cracker.
"But it's perfect
for watering radishes.
Just fill the bucket
with water
and walk down
the row of radishes.
The water will dribble out
just where you want it."

"You don't grow radishes,"
says Fletcher.
"I'm the one who grows radishes."

"Well, I guess you're right,"
says Cracker.
"I'll let you have it
for thirty cents."

"Sold!" says Fletcher.

"I'll let you have
this broken hoe for nothing,
if you can figure out
what it's good for,"
says Cracker.
He gave the hoe a kick.

Fletcher looked at it,
picked it up
and looked at it some more.
"It's no good," he says.
"Needs a new handle.
Might as well get a new hoe."

"This broken hoe will make
a perfect something-else,"
says Cracker.
"For forty cents
I'll tell you what it is."

"Sold!" says Fletcher. "What is it?"

"Foot scraper," says Cracker.
"You nail it down next to your door
  so you can scrape the mud
  off your feet
  before you go in."

"That's just what I need!"
says Fletcher.

"That's just what you got,"
says Cracker.
"Now, then . . ."
He picked up the umbrella.

"Not much to do with that,"
says Fletcher.
"The ribs are broken."

"You're right," says Cracker.
"It's a dead umbrella. But . . ."

"But what?" says Fletcher.
"You can't fix it."

"If we tore it apart,"
  says Cracker,
"the shaft would make a dandy cane."

"Right!" says Fletcher. "I'll take it!"

"There's more," says Cracker.
"You can use the cloth part
  for a birdcage cover."

"I'll take that, too!" says Fletcher.

honk, honk, honk, honk, honk, honk, honk."

"Hold on," says Cracker.
"Do you have a birdcage?"

"I'll get one," says Fletcher.
"How much for the umbrella?"

"I'll throw it in for nothing,"
  says Cracker.
"As it is, you owe me a dollar even."

"All this stuff for only a dollar?"
  says Fletcher.
He passed the dollar
  over to Cracker.

"Well, no," says Cracker.
"Let's just say the stuff's for free.
  The dollar's for the education."

take the garbage out george
the garbage man is coming
in the morning
n' if it aint out
you gonna get up
in the mornin'
ta put it out
so get up
from in front of
that t.v. n'
put the garbage out

dont spill none of
it either
george

A POEM BY GEORGE BUGGS

33

Johnnie Crack and Flossie Snail
Kept their baby in a milking pail
Flossie Snail and Johnnie Crack
One would pull it out and one would put it back.

O it's my turn now said Flossie Snail
To take the baby from the milking pail
And it's my turn now said Johnnie Crack
To smack it on the head and put it back.

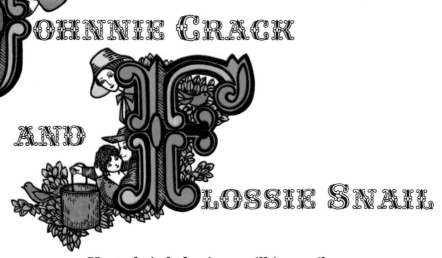

JOHNNIE CRACK
AND FLOSSIE SNAIL

Kept their baby in a milking pail
One would put it back and one would pull it out
And all it had to drink was ale and stout
For Johnnie Crack and Flossie Snail
Always used to say that stout and ale
Was *good* for a baby in a milking pail.

A POEM BY DYLAN THOMAS,
DECORATIVE LETTERING BY BETTY FRASER

Speak Roughly

to your little boy,
and beat him
when he sneezes;
he only does it
to annoy,
because he knows
it teases.
wow!
wow!
wow!

A POEM BY LEWIS CARROLL

Carlyle Cornerstone was only 5½ years old,
but already he held the speed record for tricycles.
Carlyle's goal was to make it
around the block on Normal Street
in less than one minute flat.
To increase his speed,
Carlyle leaned over the handlebars like a horse jockey,
he took the fenders off,
and he oiled the wheels 15 times a day.

As he sped along the sidewalk,
Carlyle talked to his tricycle.

Jing! Jing! Go Spirit of Kool Aid! Faster, Boy! Jing! Jing!

Everyone on Normal Street looked both ways
before crossing the sidewalk.
Nobody knew when "Jing! Jing! Faster Boy! Faster!
'Spirit of Kool Aid!' Jing! Jing!"
might run them down on the sidewalk.
Even the dogs, cats and squirrels
had learned to be cautious.

KEEP OFF
THE GRASS

Carlyle roared around the block day after day,
but he was not alone in his travels.
Mr. Teacup always rode with him...
but no one ever saw Mr. Teacup.
He was invisible.

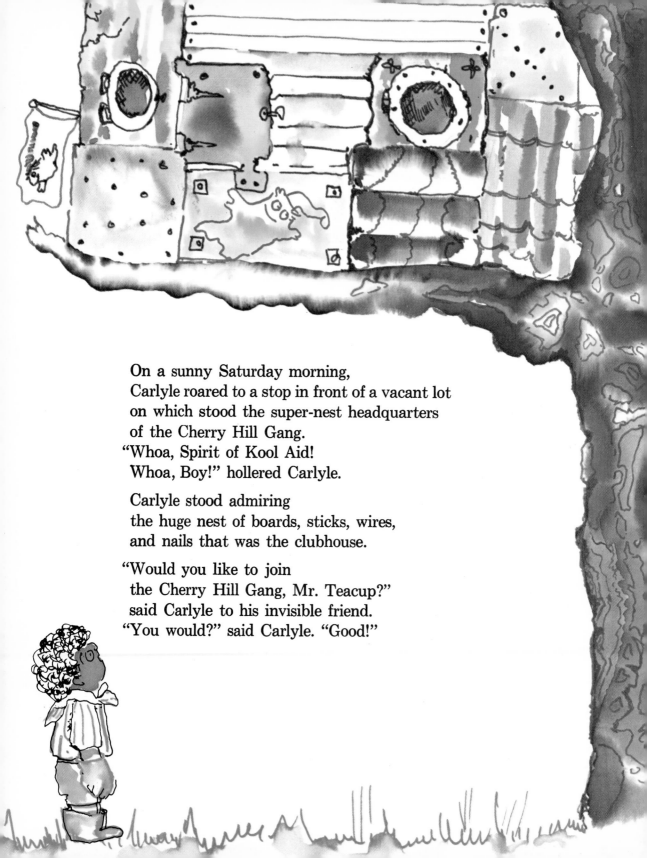

On a sunny Saturday morning,
Carlyle roared to a stop in front of a vacant lot
on which stood the super-nest headquarters
of the Cherry Hill Gang.
"Whoa, Spirit of Kool Aid!
Whoa, Boy!" hollered Carlyle.

Carlyle stood admiring
the huge nest of boards, sticks, wires,
and nails that was the clubhouse.

"Would you like to join
the Cherry Hill Gang, Mr. Teacup?"
said Carlyle to his invisible friend.
"You would?" said Carlyle. "Good!"

"You first, Mr. Teacup!" said Carlyle.
Carlyle and his invisible friend
climbed the ladder to the clubhouse
and found Freddy, Scarlet, and Shooey
playing rummy in the bottom of the nest.
Spiro, Freddy's rooster,
sat on a tiny, battery-powered turntable.

"Hello there!" said Carlyle.
"Can I join your club?"
"No!" replied Freddy.
"Can Mr. Teacup join?" said Carlyle.
"Who?" replied Freddy.
"Meet Mr. Teacup!" said Carlyle who pointed to thin air.
"How do you do, Mr. Teacup?"
 said Freddy who strained to see behind Carlyle.

"Uh . . . I don't think I see Mr. Teacup," said Freddy.
"Don't worry, he's here,
 you just can't see him or hear him,
 but I can," said Carlyle.
"Carlyle Cornerstone, you are nuts!" said Scarlet.
"Whaddaya mean?" hollered Carlyle.
"What's nuts about my friend!"

PLEASE, Scarlet, mind your manners,

said Freddy
who stared curiously in search of Mr. Teacup.
"How might we get a peep at Mr. Teacup?" asked Freddy.

"Be his friend and believe in him," replied Carlyle.

"Listen, Carlyle Cornerstone," said Scarlet,
"let's not be icky about this!
 You know perfectly well that nobody—
 but *nobody* is standing where you say a man is!
 If we can't see him, then he's *nobody*!"

"He is *too* somebody!" wailed Carlyle.

Now....now Carlyle, we believe he's there, and he can be a member of our club too!

said Freddy.

Freddy's eyes strained at the invisible man,
and deep in Freddy's scientific eyes
glimmered the raving glow
of the ghost hunter.
Freddy knew right then and there
that if there really was a Mr. Teacup,
Freddy Freon would get a look at him—or it.

Carlyle said, "Thank you for allowing
Mr. Teacup and me to join the gang.
We must go now.
We've got a race coming up."
Carlyle and Mr. Teacup
climbed down the ladder out of the nest.

Nice to have
met you, Mr. Teacup!

hollered Freddy.

He's happy
to have met
you too!

hollered back Carlyle.

Freddy's face was deeply fixed in thought.

"You don't really believe his ravings
about Mr. Teacup, do you?"asked Scarlet.

"Carlyle is a normal kid," replied Freddy.
"Most everybody talks to himself now and then."

"Does everyone have an invisible friend?" asked Shooey.

"I suppose not," replied Freddy, "but I have a feeling
that somehow there may be more to Carlyle's Mr. Teacup
than just thin air.
And if he is real,
I'm going to catch him!"

On Saturday morning,
Freddy marched to his electric room
to build an electric ghost trap.
He lugged an old over-stuffed chair
up the stairs from the garage.
He replaced the stuffing with a weird assortment
of wires, cogs, gears, bulbs, springs, switches and tubes.
He wired and soldered,
and at last finished making an electric ghost trap chair.

Mr. Freon looked cautiously at the electric chair
which was covered with switches, dials, straps and wires.
"That's a ghost trap?" he asked.

"It certainly is!" replied Freddy.
"That chair will catch anything that sits in it.
Sit down in it and you'll see how it works!"

Mr. Freon bravely closed his eyes,
crossed his fingers,
and sat down in the electric ghost trap chair.
Instantly, straps popped into place
around Mr. Freon's waist, arms, legs and neck.
Lights flashed and buzzers buzzed.

"Certainly!" replied Freddy. "That's the easy part!
You get to be the first to test my new invention
to pop people out of chairs!"

WAIT!
I don't want
to test your
people
popper!

But it was too late.
Freddy had already punched
the people popper button on the electric chair.

The straps popped off Mr. Freon.
A huge spring under the seat sprang into action.

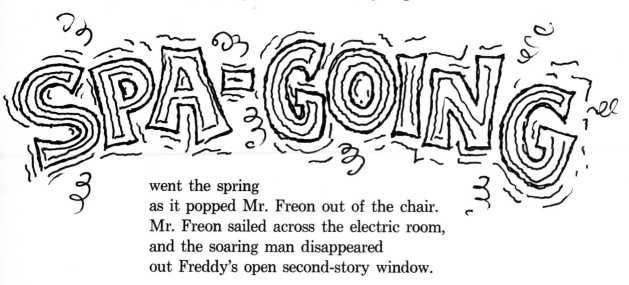

SPA-GOING

went the spring
as it popped Mr. Freon out of the chair.
Mr. Freon sailed across the electric room,
and the soaring man disappeared
out Freddy's open second-story window.

Freddy rushed to the open window and he looked out.

Mr. Freon lay on his back in the fishpond.
Mrs. Freon's head popped out the front door.
"Oh for gracious-sakes, Albert!"
She bustled about the lawn
tossing the goldfish back into the fishpond.

Knowing now that the electric ghost trap chair was successful,
Freddy waited on the sidewalk for Carlyle.
Within a few minutes, "Jing! Jing! Go, Spirit of Kool Aid!
Faster Boy! Faster!" sounded
and Carlyle roared around the corner
and screeched to a stop in front of Freddy's house.

"I have a surprise for Mr. Teacup
in my electric room," said Freddy.

"I like surprises!
And so does Mr. Teacup!" said Carlyle
as the two boys and the ghostly Mr. Teacup
raced upstairs to the electric room.

"There's the surprise!" said Freddy,
and he pointed proudly to the electric chair.

Carlyle stared at the chair.
"What's that thing?" he asked.

"A chair I made especially for Mr. Teacup,"
replied Freddy.
"Mr. Teacup, please be seated."

"How nice of you to make a chair for my friend,"
said Carlyle.

"Do you like the chair?" said Carlyle to Mr. Teacup.
"You do?"
He says it's the most comfortable chair he's ever sat in,"
said Carlyle to Freddy.

Freddy stared at the empty chair where the ghost sat resting.
No lights flashed, no buzzers buzzed,
and no straps popped into place.

"He certainly must be a very thin ghost!" muttered Freddy.

"Thin as air!" replied Carlyle.

"Where does Mr. Teacup go at night?" asked Freddy,
now convinced that the electric ghost trap chair
would not catch a ghost.

"He sleeps outside in the driveway
on top of our station wagon," replied Carlyle.

"Why does he sleep on top of a station wagon?"
asked Freddy.

"Where would you sleep
if you were 7 feet, 9 inches tall?"
asked Carlyle.

"On top of a station wagon, I suppose," muttered Freddy.

Carlyle and Mr. Teacup left the electric room
to continue roaring around the block,
and the determined Freddy Freon
made plans to catch a sleeping ghost.

In the early evening hours of May 15th,
Freddy puttered in the electric room
getting ready for a night ghost-hunt
after Mr. Teacup was asleep on the station wagon next door.
But nobody, not even a scientist,
goes ghost-hunting by himself,
so Freddy invited Shooey Madera
over for an evening of "fun and games."

At 7:15 p.m., Shooey entered Freddy's electric room.
"What are we going to do tonight, Freddy,
play dominoes?" said Shooey.

"We're going ghost-hunting!" replied Freddy
who busily cut eye-holes in an old sheet.

"But I'm afraid of ghosts!" exclaimed Shooey.

Freddy cut eye-holes in another old sheet.
"No ghost will get us,
because we'll be ghosts ourselves!" said Freddy,
and he slipped the sheet over his head.

He draped the other over Shooey.

Freddy cut tiny eye-holes in a pillow case
and covered Spiro.
The rooster ghost strutted out of the electric room
behind Freddy and Shooey.

"Please be home by eight o'clock, boys," said Mrs. Freon
as the three ghosts fluttered down the stairs.

Crickets sang in the grass
and a big yellow moon hung over the tree tops
as the ghost hunters sneaked toward the station wagon
parked in the Cornerstone driveway.

"FF...FF...FF...FF...Freddy!" whispered Shooey,
"What do we do if the ghost catches us
instead of us catching him?"

"We run!" whispered Freddy.

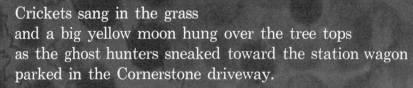

With the rooter under a pillow case tagging along behind,
the two boys crept through the shrubs and bushes
to the station wagon.

"I'm going to get a picture of Mr. Teacup with my camera,"
whispered Freddy,
who climbed up a tree beside the driveway
and hung by his knees from a limb over the station wagon.

Freddy made his camera ready to snap a picture.

But ever so quietly,
the Cornerstone front door slowly opened.
Mr. Cornerstone silently slipped outside.
He saw Shooey and Spiro
beside the station wagon
and Freddy hanging from the limb.

BURGLARS!

Every porch light on Normal Street flashed on.

"Maaaaaaaaaaaaaa!!" screamed Shooey
as he raced madly down the sidewalk toward home.

Spiro screeched and ran.

The flashbulb in Freddy's camera
popped in Mr. Cornerstone's face
and Freddy slipped from the limb and fell.

Mr. Cornerstone staggered about the lawn
blinded by the flashbulb,
with Freddy struggling to get out of the sheet.

Mr. Freon burst out from his front door
to see what all the howling, hollering,
and yowling was about.
He raced madly across the front lawn
and plunged head-long into the fishpond.

He staggered out of the pool wet and dripping,
only to run head-on into Mr. Cornerstone.

"Thunderation!" shrieked Mr. Cornerstone
as the struggling mass of men fell once again
into the fishpool with a tremendous splash.

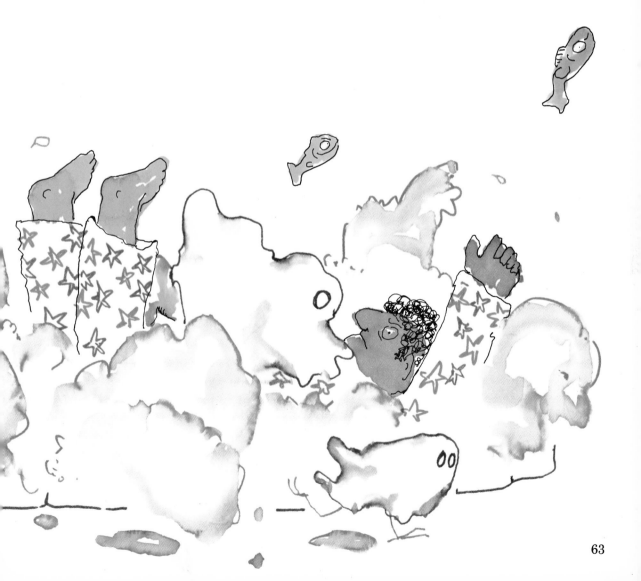

Freddy raced up the stairs to the electric room
to save his wet film.

All the porch lights on Normal Street slowly went out,
and Spiro strutted back home
to his turntable in the electric room.

Freddy emerged from his darkroom closet
with a dripping wet photograph
which he held up to the light.
He stared at the photo
and his eyes became large
at what he saw on the print.

The next morning
Freddy carried the ghost photo out for Carlyle to see.
Soon, from around the corner, came,
"Jing! Jing! Go!
Go 'Spirit of Kool Aid!'
Faster boy! Jing Jing!"

Carlyle screeched to a stop in front of Freddy.
"Hello, Freddy!" said Carlyle pleasantly.

"Carlyle!" said Freddy.
"Look at this picture!
I got a picture of Mr. Teacup last night!"

Carlyle leaned over his handlebars
and squinted a look at the picture.
"That is only a blur in a picture," said Carlyle.
"Mr. Teacup wasn't here last night.
He's on a vacation in Florida."

"Listen, Carlyle," said Freddy,
"that really is an image of a ghost in that picture!"

Carlyle jumped on his tricycle
and started off.

"Carlyle! Come back here!" yelled Freddy.
"Mr. Teacup is a ghost,
and he really is real!
The picture shows it!"

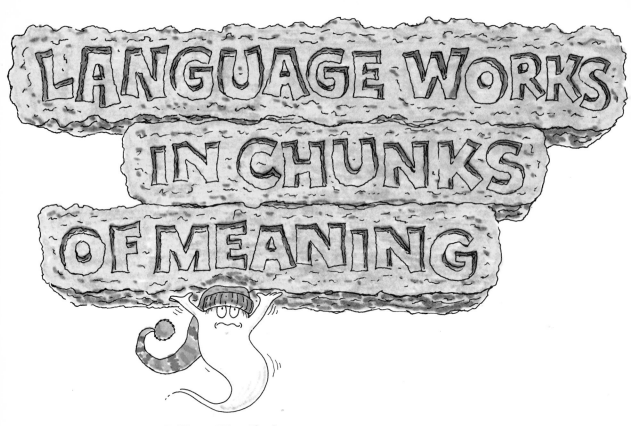

LANGUAGE WORKS IN CHUNKS OF MEANING

Bill: Noodles!
Put those chunks of language
back in your head
where they belong!

Noodles: I don't think I want to, Bill Martin.
Ghosts carry their language
on top of their heads
—or anywhere they want.
That's because we're magic.

Bill: Magic or not, Noodles,
language begins in the head
and always works in chunks.

Noodles: Chunks of what?

Bill: Chunks of meaning.
Listen to me talk, Noodles,
and hear how my words cluster.

Noodles: Clusters? You talking about peanut clusters?

Bill: Well, something like that, Noodles.
Just as peanuts are held together
by sticky chocolate
words also are held together
by the *sound of sense.*

Noodles: I think I like sticky chocolate better.

Bill: Alright, Noodles, let's test your *sound of sense.*

Noodles: There you go, Bill Martin,
talking like a school teacher.
Tests! Tests! Tests!
I like sticky chocolate better.

Bill: Then use your sticky chocolate, Noodles,
to cluster these words together
so they sound like talking:

*(Bill reads these words in monotone
with a pause between each word.
It does not sound like language.
It sounds like a long list of spelling words.)*

Once	was	rode	house	of	was	and
upon	a	a	after	himself	scared	so
a	silly	mouse	dark	in	to	was
time	ghost	through	and,	the	death	his
there	who	the	catching	mirror,		horse.
			a			
			glimpse			

Noodles: I'm glad you don't talk like that very often Bill Martin.
That sounds crazy.

Bill: You're getting the point, Noodles!
Language doesn't work like that.
What does your ear tell you to do
with those words?

Noodles: Well, my little ear tells me
to put "Once upon a time" together,
like a little song. (sings)

    Once upon a time . . .
    Once upon a time . . .

Bill: Keep going, Noodles,
your "sticky chocolate" is working.

Noodles: Give me that list of words, Bill Martin.
I'll stick 'em together the way they really belong:

    Once upon a time . . .
    there was a silly ghost . . .

Hey, I'm changing that chunk right now because it's not true . . .

    Once upon a time . . .
    there was a cool ghost . . .
    who rode a mouse . . .
    through the house . . .

No, he didn't just "ride a mouse." He rode it

    wildly through the house . . .
    after dark,
    and,
    catching a glimpse of himself in the mirror,
    said,
    "Oh, what a gallant rider!
    What a gallant steed!"

Bill: Noodles, I think you changed some of those words.

Noodles: Just a minute, Bill.
Who's putting these peanut clusters together, me or you?

Bill: Well, I can see you are, Noodles,
and I can also see that you know
how to cluster words
into the *sound of sense.*

Noodles: Yeah, Bill Martin.
I know how to do lots of things
—like getting out of here right now.
Goodbye, Bill Martin, goodbye.

Bill: Wait a minute Noodles.
I want you to help me
put this book together.
Here are two stories, *"The Ant,
the Lamb, the Cricket and the Mouse,"*
and *"To Market, To Market."*
Let's see you put them
into chunks of meaning
so that each chunk has the *sound of sense.*

Noodles: Hokus, pokus,
diddeley dokus!
Presto Chango,
Me go mego!

Bill: Noodles, finish the job before you leave.

Noodles: I already finished, Bill Martin.
Turn the page and you'll find
"The Ant, the Lamb, the Cricket and the Mouse,"
printed in chunks of meaning.

Bill: What about *"To Market, To Market?"*

Noodles: Oh, gracious, I'm too tired.
Carrying all those chunks around just wore me out.
"To Market, To Market"
will have to be done by somebody else, not me!
Goodbye, Bill Martin.
Oodeley, oodeley!

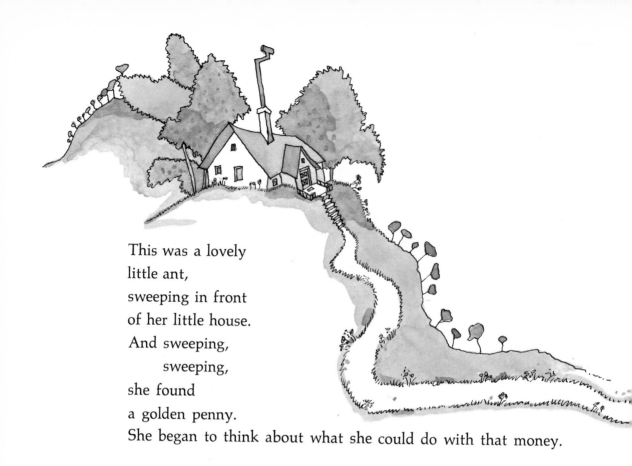

This was a lovely
little ant,
sweeping in front
of her little house.
And sweeping,
        sweeping,
she found
a golden penny.
She began to think about what she could do with that money.

the Ant
the Lamb
the Cricket
and the Mouse

A story by Anita Brenner,
pictures by Uri Shulevitz

She said,
"If I lend money at interest,
that would turn out well,
but what I am afraid of is
that my friends would come
asking me for things.
And if I start a store,
the locusts would come
and eat all the grain.
The best thing is
to buy a beautiful hat
and a lovely dress
and make myself pretty
and see if that way
somebody loves me.

Then maybe I will get married."

She bought everything
she had thought of,
as well as a beautiful
and luxurious mirror.
When she had
everything she wanted,
she dressed up
and she held up
her beautiful mirror
and looked at her
beautiful self.

She said,
"Now I am ready,"
and she went out
on the street wearing
all her new things.

As she went along,
she met some
very nice-looking lambs,
and she said
to the nicest one,
"Dear little lamb,
will you do me
the very great favor
of telling me how I look?"

He said,
"Why you look very nice,
my dear little ant."
"Oh, well,
do you know
I would like
to get married,
and this is why
I have dressed up?
Wouldn't you like
to marry me?"
"If you like,"
said the lamb,
"we will get married."
"Very well,"
said the ant.

"But let's see first,
how are you going
to talk to me?"
    "Oh,"
said the lamb.
"Beh, beh, beh."
    "No, no,"
said the ant.
"If you talk to me
like that,
I shall be frightened.
After all I don't love you,
my dear little lamb.
You can go now."

    Just then
a cricket was passing by,
and the ant told him
she wanted to get married.
    "You look so nice,"
said the cricket,
"I will certainly
marry you."

    "All right,"
said the ant,
"but first I want to know
how you are going
to talk to me."
    The cricket answered,
"Gree, gree, gree."
    Said the ant,
"I don't like
your way of talking.
It would frighten me.
So good-by, little cricket,
you can skip along."

75

"Very well,
little mouse,
but I want to know first
how you are going
to talk to me."

Now a very pretty
little mouse came by,
very nicely dressed.
And the ant said,
"Dear little mouse,
my idea is that I want
to get married,
but I have not yet
succeeded in my plan.
I think I will decide
to marry you,
dear little mouse."
    "All right,
little ant,
I accept with pleasure,"
he said.

"So you want to know
how I am going
to talk to you?
Very well,
I am going to say,
listen,
'Eeee, eeee, eeee.' "
    "Well,
that might frighen me,"
said the ant.
"It might,
but anyway
let us get married,
dear little mouse."

Some days,
the little ant would say
to the little mouse,
"I want you to go
to the market for me,
to buy all our groceries."
And he would answer,
"No, I can't go.
You go,
and I will stay home
and cook."

So they got married,

and

they were very happy.

The ant accepted
and would go to market,
but first
she would tell the mouse
what to cook
and when to put vegetables
in the soup.
And then
the little ant would go
to the market thinking
how much she loved
her little mouse.

The Snakebit Hoe-handle

From many sources in the southern Appalachians

A copperhead snake made for me
one day when I was hoein' my corn.
Happened I saw him in time,
and I lit into him with the hoe.

He thrashed around,
bit the hoe-handle a couple of times,
but I fin'lly killed him.
Hung him on the fence.

Went on back to work,
and directly my hoe-handle felt thicker'n common.
I looked it over good and it was swellin'.
The poison from that snakebite
was workin' all through it.

After I tried it a few more licks
it popped the shank and the hoe-head fell off.

So I threw that handle over by the fence;
went and fixed me another'n.

Got my corn hoed out about dark.

Week or two after that

I was lookin' over my cornfield,

and I noticed a log in the fencerow.

Examined it right close

and blame if it wasn't that hoe-handle!

Hit was swelled up big enough for lumber

So I took it and had it sawed.

Had enough boards

to build me a new chicken house.

Then I painted it and, don't you know!—

the turpentine in the paint
took out all that swellin',
and the next mornin'
my chicken house had shrunk
to the size of a shoe box.
Good thing I hadn't put my chickens in it!

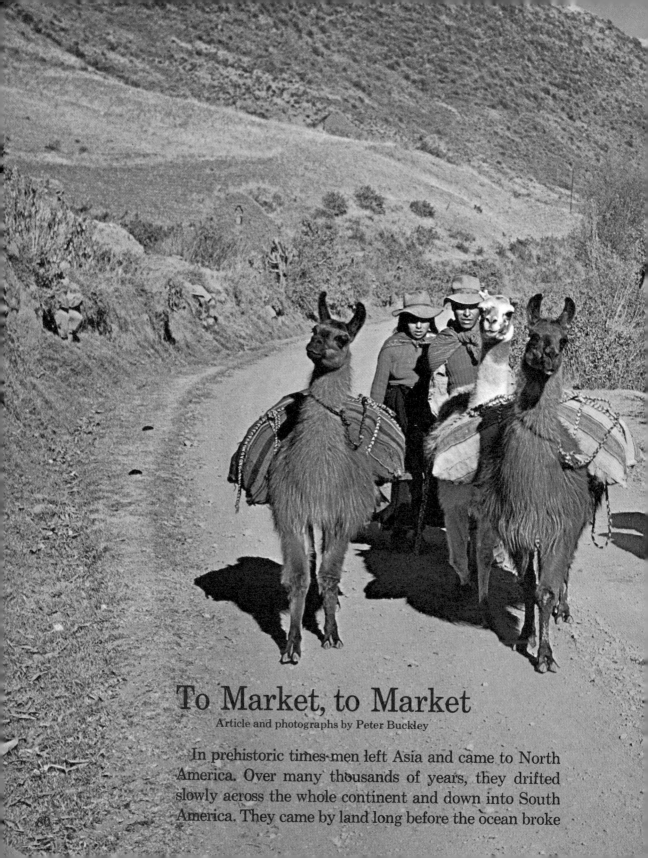

To Market, to Market

Article and photographs by Peter Buckley

In prehistoric times men left Asia and came to North America. Over many thousands of years, they drifted slowly across the whole continent and down into South America. They came by land long before the ocean broke

through and separated Asia and America. Along this same route the camel also came. The Peruvian Indians today are the descendants of the people who came from Asia, and the llama is descended from the camel. The Indians need llamas, for the llama gives them meat and wool besides carrying loads over the mountains.

The Indians work very very hard! An Indian mother on the way from her village to the market in the town of Pisac is a busy woman. She takes care of her child who is strapped tightly to her back. She watches her small herd of llamas as they walk along the mountain road carrying bags of potatoes.

Her husband dug the potatoes out of the ground in his fields yesterday, and he sheared two of his llamas for their wool.

Now, on her way to sell the potatoes, the man's wife is spinning the llama wool into the yarn which she will later use to weave a blanket. One day she will also sell the blanket in the market place at Pisac.

From many villages in the valley, and from the high mountains which rise up steeply on either side of the valley, farmers and their wives come twice a week to the market in Pisac.

The people dress differently in the different villages, and so it is very easy to know where a person lives simply by looking at his hat.

In the villages there are no stores; and so if a man wants to sell his fruits and vegetables or if his wife wants to buy some cloth, they must come to town.

Early in the morning it is cold. Before the sun rises above the snow-capped Andes, before the people arrive, the market place is swept clean. When the people reach Pisac, they carefully spread their goods out in front of them and wait for someone to buy.

Nowhere can you see a price tag. Everyone bargains for a long time before buying or selling. The woman who wants to buy a blanket hopes to pay as little as possible for it. The woman who is selling the blanket hopes to receive as much as possible for it. It takes time to agree on a price which is acceptable to both women, and it takes time to exchange news with friends.

By noon the marketing is over, and everyone is ready to start the long walk home. Once again, the llamas are loaded. The woman who sold her husband's potatoes in the market has in turn bought oranges. She has fed her child in Pisac with the food she brought with her, and now the child is asleep on her back.

Before the people leave, however, an orchestra appears in the market place. Everybody gathers to listen to the music.

After a while three men, wearing masks and costumes, begin to dance to the music.

This is the only entertainment enjoyed by the Indians near Pisac, for they have no movies, no television, and no theater. Only a very few people own small battery-operated radios. If the batteries die, they cannot plug in their radios, for there is no electricity in most villages.

Many people who have no business to do in the market come to enjoy the music and the dancing. They stand very straight and very still while they listen and watch.

On market day in Pisac, it is very hard to believe that Spanish soldiers conquered the Indians in Peru over four hundred years ago.

The language which the people speak today is Quechua, the language spoken long before the Spanish came. The music and the dancing are Indian. The clothes the people wear are Indian. Even the food which the people eat today is the Indian food eaten long before the conquest.

The Indians grew many things which the rest of the world never saw before Columbus discovered America. A thousand years ago they ate corn, potatoes, peanuts, tomatoes, strawberries and chocolate, and a thousand years ago they sold these things in open-air markets. When the Spanish came, they were amazed to see these new foods.

By midafternoon on market day in Pisac, the town is quiet. The musicians and the dancers are gone. The market place is empty.

On the road which leads down the valley and on the paths in the high mountains, the people are urging their llamas toward home.

In a few days they will return to Pisac on another market day.

USING YOUR EARS IN READING

Noodles:	Oodeley, oodeley, little ear, Are you readin' what you hear?
Bill:	Good morning, Noodles.
Noodles:	Don't bother me, Bill Martin. I'm reading... With my ears.
Bill:	Everybody reads partly with his ears.
Noodles:	My ears are busy, Bill Martin. They're reading.
Bill:	Reading what?
Noodles:	Words! Words! Words! This is a mess!
Bill:	I don't see any words on that page, Noodles.
Noodles:	The words are invisible...just for ghosts...like me. So just listen:

Words, Words

A POEM BY ILO ORLEANS

Many words
That sound alike
Mean different things —
 Like these:
Tail and tale,
And pail and pale
And sees and seize
 And seas.

And deer and dear,
And hear and here,
And two and to
 And too,
And pear and pair,
And fare and fair,
And dew and due
 And do.

Many words
That sound alike
Mean different things
 I know;
Like son and sun,
And one and won,
And sew and sow
 And so.

Noodles: I can tell you one thing, Bill Martin,
our language is crazy.
Look at these *words.*
How can anybody read this mess?
Wer-dz! Wer-dz! Wer-dz!
Oh, little ear,
you are my teacher, my dear teacher.
Without you, dear ear, my eye would
be in a slug of trouble.

Bill: No doubt.

Noodles: Be careful with your silent b's, Bill Martin.
My ear doesn't hear them.

Bill: But your ear knows to skip over them
and tells your eyes to do the same.

Noodles: My *nose* has nothing to do with it.
It's my ears!

Bill:	That's what I said.
Noodles:	My *eyes* said it too.
Bill:	So we're agreed.
Noodles:	Yes, I think.
Bill:	On what!
Noodles:	The eyes cannot read anything the ears have not heard.
Bill:	Robert Frost said that.
Noodles:	So did I. And now I'm going to test your ears, Bill Martin.
Bill:	I thought you didn't like tests.
Noodles:	For you they're okay, Bill Martin. Four me their knot sew good. Hear, reed this:

One, Two, Three – Gough!

To make some bread you must have dough,
Isn't that sough?

If the sky is clear all through,
Is the color of it blough?

When is the time to put your hand to the plough?
Nough!

The handle on the pump near the trough
Nearly fell ough.

Bullies sound rough and tough enough,
But you can often call their blough.

BY EVE MERRIAM

Bill:	Touché! Nudlz, u'v mayed yor poynt.
Noodles:	Aye thinque aisle gow nau, Bil Mar'n.
Bill:	Doughn't luz yure eerz, Newduhlz. U nede them evrie tiem yeau reed. Thuh speling uv wirdz in hour langwidge sometimes can be counted on to tell us how to pronounce them, but other times—Waugh!— thuh speling iz a mishmash uhntil thee ier goze tu werk.
Noodles:	Gouldbigh! Gudbahee.
Bill:	Noodles, your confusing me.
Noodles:	Then trust your ears. Goodbye, Bill. Oodeley! Oodeley.

Bill:	Eye'll never be the same.

archie the cockroach
climbed upon a typewriter
one night
and found a paper in the machine
all ready for typing
so he jumped around the keys
to spell out this message
for humans

doing well

as i was
crawling through
a shoe store the
other day i
heard two pairs of shoes
talking to each other

well says the
first pair
you neednt feel
so smart
you have been
marked down from
twenty dollars to sixteen
while i have been marked
down from twenty one
dollars to
eighteen dollars
well said the
second pair i
make no claims to
superiority but
i will say i think
we are both doing
mighty well for
five dollar shoes

from *the lives and times of archy
and mehitabel* by don marquis

ADVICE TO A BIRD, SPECIES UNKNOWN

Listen to me, you silly bird,
Has no one told you?
        Haven't you heard
That the winters here are long and cold?
Then harken, bird. You are being told.
Be on your way!
      Go south!
        Get going!
Any time now it may be snowing,
Sleet and hail and a mean wind blowing.
Winter is here.
       Didn't you know that?
And winter's a crusty old gray cat,
Ice on his whiskers,
      frost on his paws.
He'll gobble you up in his freezing jaws!
He'll snap you up in his arctic mouth!
I'm telling you, bird,
     be bright,
       GO SOUTH!

A POEM BY GEORGE STARBUCK GALBRAITH,
LETTERING BY FRANK ALOISE

TAILYPO

AN OLD NEGRO TALE

PITCHERS AND LETTERN BY RAY BARBER

Once upon a time,
way down in de big woods of Tennessee,
dey lived a man all by hisself.
His house didn't hab but one room in it,
an dat room was his parlor,
his settin room, his bedroom,
his dinin room an his kitchen, too.
In one end of de room was a great, big,
open fireplace, an dat's whar
de man cooked an et his supper.

An one night atter he had cooked
an et his supper, dey crep in troo
de cracks of the logs de curiestes creetur
dat you ebber did see, an it had
a GREAT, BIG, LONG TAIL.
Jis as soon as dat man see dat varmint,
he reached fur his hatchet,
an wid one lick, he cut dat thing's tail off.
De creatur crep out troo de cracks
of de logs an run away, an de man,
fool like, he took an cooked dat tail,
he did, an he et it.

Den he went ter bed, an atter a while, he went ter sleep. He hadn't been sleep berry long, till he waked up, an heerd sumpin climbin up de side of his cabin. It sounded jis like a cat, an he could heer it

SCRATCH, SCRATCH, SCRATCH,

an by an by, he heerd it say,

"TAILYPO, TAILYPO;
ALL I WANT'S MY TAILYPO."

Now dis yeer man had tree dawgs: one wuz called uno, an one wuz called ino, an de udder one wuz called cumptico-calico. An when he heerd dat thing he called his dawgs,

HUH! HUH! HUH!

An dem dawgs cum bilin out from under de floor, an dey chased dat thing way down in de big woods. An der man went back ter bed an went ter sleep.

Well, way long in de middle of de night, he waked up an he heerd sumpin right above his cabin door, tryin ter git in. He listened, an he could heer it

SCRATCH, SCRATCH, SCRATCH,
an den he heerd it say,

"TAILYPO, TAILYPO;
ALL I WANT'S MY TAILYPO."

An he sot up in bed and called his dawgs,
HUH! HUH! HUH!
An dem dawgs cum bustin round de corner
of de house an dey cotched up wid dat thing
at de gate an dey jis tore de whole fence
down, tryin ter git at it. An dat time,
dey chased it way down in de big swamp.
An de man went back ter bed agin
an went ter sleep.

Way long toward mornin he waked up,
an he heerd sumpin down in de big swamp.
He listened, an heerd it say,

"YOU KNOW, I KNOW;
ALL I WANT'S MY TAILYPO!"

An dat man sot up in bed all called his dawgs,
HUH! HUH! HUH!
An you know dat time dem dawgs didn cum.
Dat thing had carried em way off down
in de big swamp an killed em, or lost em.

An de man went back ter bed, an went
ter sleep agin.

Well, jis before daylight he waked up
an he heerd sumpin an it sounded like a cat,
climbin up de civers at de foot of his bed.
He listened an he could heer it
SCRATCH, SCRATCH, SCRATCH,
an he looked ober the foot of his bed
an he saw two little pinted ears,
an in a minute, he saw two big,
round firey eyes lookin at him.
He wanted to call his dawgs,
but he too skeered ter holler.
Dat thing kep creepin up until by an by,
it wuz right on top of dat man,
an den it said in a low voice,

"TAILYPO, TAILYPO;
ALL I WANT'S MY TAILYPO."
An all at once dat man got his voice
an he said, "I hain't got your TAILYPO!"
An dat thing said,"Oh, yes, you has,...
And I'm gonna GET IT!"

Mairzy Doats

Mairzy Doats and Dozy Doats
And liddle lamzy divey
A kiddley divey too, wouldn't you?

Yes! Mairzy Doats and Dozy Doats
And liddle lamzy divey
A kiddley divey too, wouldn't you?

If the words sound queer,

and funny to your ear,

a little bit jumbled and jivey,

Sing, "Mares eat oats and does eat oats

and little lambs eat ivy."

Oh! Mairzy Doats and Dozy Doats

And liddle lamzy divey

A kiddley divey too, wouldn't you-oo?

A kiddley divey too, wouldn't you?

Words and music by
Milton Drake,
Al Hoffman,
Jerry Livingston

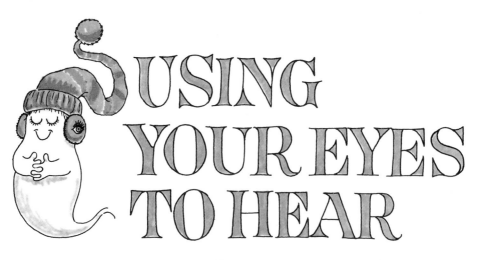

USING YOUR EYES TO HEAR

Bill: Noodles, are those earmuffs?

Noodles: Speak a little louder, Bill.
I can't hear you.

Bill: I said, WHY ARE YOU WEARING EARMUFFS?

Noodles: I think I can't hear you.

Bill: WHY THE EARMUFFS?

Noodles: Bill Martin, you don't talk very good sometimes.

Bill: TAKE OFF THOSE EARMUFFS, NOODLES!

Noodles: I'll take them off, Bill Martin,
but why are you shouting?

Bill: I'm sorry, Noodles.
I was trying to make you hear.

Noodles: It won't work, Bill. Today I'm just listening with my eyes.

Bill: That's a good reading skill, Noodles.
I didn't know you knew so much about reading.

Noodles: I know many, many things
that you don't know I know, Bill Martin.

Bill: That's true, Noodles.
Each one of us carries a lot of knowledge in our heads
that even we don't know we have.

Noodles: I'm filled with knowledge.
Didn't you know that?

Bill: Yes, Noodles, you're a very knowledgeable ghost.
Now tell me more about listening with your eyes.

Noodles: Well, Bill Martin,
if you had written down what you just said,
I would have known you were shouting.

Bill: You would have?

Noodles: Sure, because the letters would have gotten bigger
and blacker and louder all the time.

Bill: Not everybody writes in big black letters
to signal that he's shouting.

Noodles: The funny papers always do.
That's why they're smarter.
School books aren't that smart, I don't think.
They just go on and on and on and on
in the same old type, forever.
All I know is I'd rather read words on a cereal box
that snap, crackle and pop!

Bill: Granted, Noodles.
It's exciting to see type explode on the page,
but a reader finds other kinds of clues
to help him hear the sounds of spoken language.

Noodles: And shouted language!

Bill: An exclamation point can tell that a sentence is shouted
even if the letters all stay the same size.

Noodles: Then you keep the exclamation points, Bill Martin,
and I'll keep the big letters.

Bill: A period signals to your eyes that a sentence is ending.
If you listen to yourself reading aloud, Noodles,
you'll hear your voice bring the flow of words
to a rest—to a stopping place.

Noodles: You don't use enough periods, Bill Martin.
You just talk and talk and talk and never stop.
That's why I'm putting my earmuffs back on.
I'd rather listen to myself.

Bill: Well, let your eyes listen to this, Noodles.

WHOSE IZZY IZZY?
IZZY YOURS OR IZZY MINE?
I'M GETTING DIZZY
WATCHIN' IZZY ALL THE TIME.
SAID HE'D MARRY ME THIS SPRING.
NOW HE'S BUYING YOU THE RING!
WHOSE IZZY IZZY?
IZZY YOURS OR IZZY MINE?

Noodles: (reads) Whose Izzy is he?
Is he yours
or is he mine?
I'm gettin'.....
Say, Bill Martin,
I like it better this way:

WHOSE ISHY ISHY?
ISHY HIS OR ISHY MINE?
I'M GETTIN' WISHY
WATCHIN' ISHY ALL THE TIME.
SAID SHE'D MARRY ME THIS SPRING,
NOW SHE'S WEARIN' IZZY'S RING.
WHOSE ISHY ISHY?
ISHY HIS OR ISHY MINE?

Goodbye, Bill Martin.
Ishy is calling me, I think.
Maybe she's changed her mind.
Oodeley, oodeley.

Bill: Goodbye, Noodles.

Mud in the road and wind in my hair,
Mud in the road and I don't care,
Snow in the shadows, but the fields are all bare,
**And a big black crow
is cawing.**

Pussy willows close to the bough,
Catkins swinging and greening now,
Chickens feeling perky and kicking up a row,
**And a big black crow
is cawing.**

Sap buckets hanging
    on our sugar maple tree,
Wild things stirring
    where no one can see,
I'm waiting for what's
    going to happen to me —

AND A BIG
BLACK
CROW
IS CAWING.

A POEM BY ELIZABETH COATSWORTH

THE ANSWER IS "NO"

What answer maketh the crow?
Always **No.**
Put several questions in a row
To a crow,
You will get **No, no, no,**
Or **No, no, no, no.**
Sometimes, on being questioned,
The crow says **Naw.**
                    Or **Caw.**
But regardless of pronunciation,
There is never anything but opposition, denial,
And negation
In a crow.
In their assemblies at the edge of town,
Crows introduce resolutions, then vote them down.
How many times in summer, waked early by the mosquito,
Have I lain listening to the crow's loud veto!
Once, gunning, I wounded a thieving
Crow
And have not forgotten his terrible, disbelieving
Oh, no!

A POEM BY E. B. WHITE

PICTURE BY BERNARD MARTIN

HOW TO
BRUSH
YOUR
TEETH

Pictures by Mel Hunter

W hen you brush your teeth,

it matters how you hold your brush. The movement

Hold the brush "bristles up" for the starting position. Do not place the brush too high on the gums.

of the brush can  massage the gum tissue

at the same time it cleans the teeth. Brushing

Turn the handle to brush downward. This massages the gums and forces the bristles between the teeth.

properly is not  an easy thing to do,

but once you have the knack of it and realize how

Continue turning the brush a complete 90°. An upward movement is used for brushing the lower teeth.

important it is,  you'll find the effort

worth your while. You have six surfaces to think

about in brushing

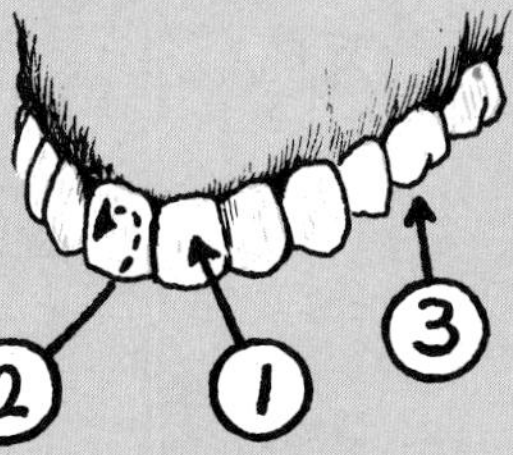

The areas of the upper teeth to be cleaned are 1) outside, 2) inside, 3) biting edge.

your teeth. First, the

outside surface of your upper teeth; second, the

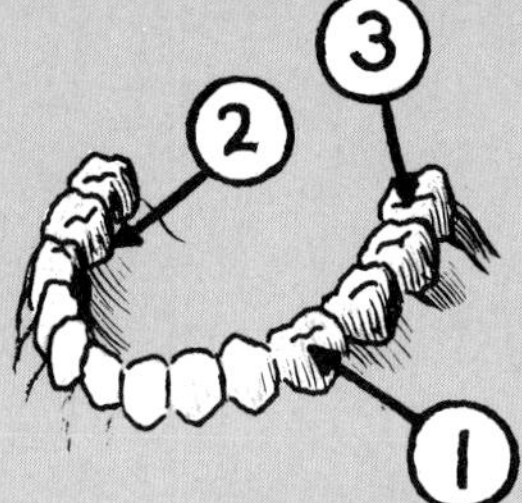

The same three areas of the lower teeth need careful cleaning: 1) outside, 2) inside, 3) biting edge.

inside surface of these teeth; third, the

grinding surfaces of the upper teeth. The next three

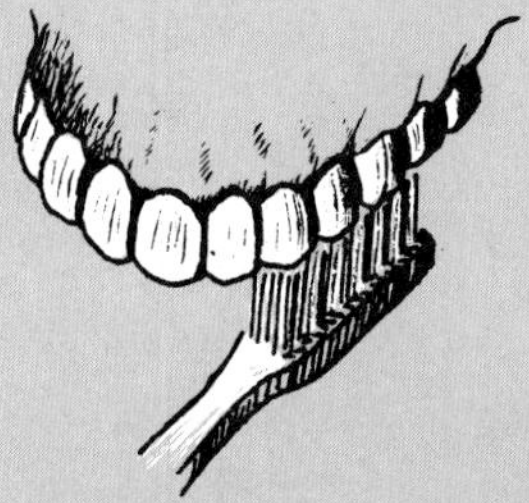

Use a back-and-forth brushing motion to clean the biting surfaces of the upper and then the lower teeth.

surfaces to clean are the similar areas

of the teeth in your lower jaw. Pictured here are

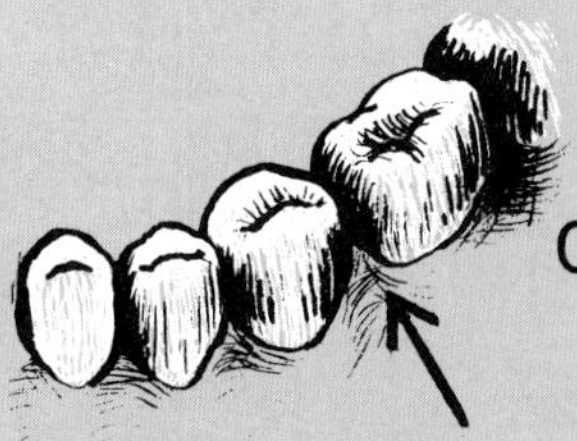

If you can't brush after eating, swish water through the spaces between your teeth.

guides for good care of your mouth. If

you spend enough time when brushing to do the job

Since your smile is an important part of your personality, it pays to take care of your teeth.

well, you'll be rewarded in years ahead.

SONG OF THE

POP-BOTTLERS

by Morris Bishop

POP BOTTLES POP-BOTTLES
IN POP SHOPS;
THE POP-BOTTLES POP BOTTLES
POOR POP DROPS.

WHEN POP DROPS POP-BOTTLES
POP-BOTTLES PLOP!
POP-BOTTLE-TOPS TOPPLE!
POP MOPS SLOP!

STOP! POP'LL DROP BOTTLE!
STOP, POP, STOP!
WHEN POP BOTTLES POP-BOTTLES,
POP-BOTTLES POP!

POP! GOES THE WEASEL

AN OLD AMERICAN SINGING GAME

A penny for a spool of thread,
A penny for a needle,
That's the way the money goes,

POP

goes the weasel!

All around the cobbler's bench
The monkey chased the weasel,
The monkey thought 'twas all in fun,

POP

goes the weasel!

USING LITERARY STRUCTURE IN READING

Bill:	Noodles, what are you doing now?
Noodles:	I'm building a story.
Bill:	What's your story about?
Noodles:	Three skunks. The little bitty skunk, the middle-size skunk and the big skunk. They really have a problem.
Bill:	Well, that sounds like a story for sure.
Noodles:	This story has a big problem, Bill Martin. You see, the skunks have to get over the hill to eat garbage.
Bill:	Well, that's no problem. Skunks know how to get over a hill.
Noodles:	I know that but you don't know what lives under the hill. That's the problem.
Bill:	Go on.

Noodles: A great big troll lives under the hill
and he won't let the skunks cross over.

Bill: Noodles, this sounds like a story I heard before.
"The Three Billy-Goats Gruff."

Noodles: Yes, but when you like a story, Bill Martin,
you can make another like it. It's so easy.
You ought to try it sometime, Bill.

Bill: Well, let's hear more about the skunks.

Noodles: Well, the little skunk went trip-trapping up the hill.
And the troll said, "No you don't, little skunk.
I'm going to eat you up."
The little skunk began to cry,
"Oh, don't eat me, Mr. Troll.
Wait for my brother.
He's fatter."
"Very well," said the troll.

"I'll wait for your brother."
So the little skunk crossed
over the hill to eat garbage.

Bill: Then what happened?

Noodles: I don't have to tell you about the second skunk, Bill Martin.
You already know, don't you?

Bill: If your story goes like other stories,
I already know how the second episode goes.
The second skunk meets the troll
and convinces him to wait for his brother.

Noodles: "Very well," said the troll.
"I'll wait for your brother.
He's the fattest of all."
And the second skunk crossed over the hill.
to eat garbage.

Bill: And now comes the third skunk.

Noodles: Yes, here comes the third skunk trip-trapping up the hill.
Trip, trap! Trip, trap!
Trip, trap! Trip, trap!
And the old troll calls out,
"Who's that crossing over my hill?"
The big billy goat—oh, I mean the big skunk said,
"It is I, the big skunk!
I'm crossing over the hill to eat garbage."
"Not by the hair of my chinny-chin-chin!"
said the troll.
And he came up out of his hole.
"Now, I'm going to eat you up!"

Bill: Go on, Noodles.
This is a good story.

Noodles: Well, that skunk
didn't have a fatter brother
so he just yelled at the troll,
"Well, come along!
I've got two spears
and I'll poke your eyeballs
out at your ears!
I've got besides two curling stones
and I'll crush you to bits—
body and bones."

Bill: Then what?

Noodles: Oh, Bill, you know.
The big skunk stinked him good!
How else would you get rid of a troll
if you were a skunk?

Bill: That got rid of the problem, all right.

Noodles: Yes, the story's done
and the problem's all over.
Goodbye, Bill.
Oodeley, oodeley!

Bill: You know, boys and girls,
that ghost never ceases to amaze me.
Where did *he* learn that you can take the pattern of a story
to create another one.

Noodles: One more thing, Bill Martin.
If you wonder how I can read stories so easy,
even when I can't sound out all the words,
it's because I can figure out
how the author put his story together.
When you can tell what he's doing,
it makes the reading so easy
you don't even worry about the big words.

Bill: Noodles, you're just a con man.
Right now you're probably figuring out
how this next story is put together.

Noodles: Not me, Bill Martin.
I'm leaving.
I think Ishy is calling me.
Oodeley, oodeley!

Sody Sallyraytus

A mountain tale collected and
written down by Richard Chase,
pictures by William Pappas

One time
there was an old woman
and an old man
and a little girl
and a little boy—
and a pet squirrel
sittin' up on the fireboard.

And one day
the old woman wanted
to bake some biscuits
but she didn't have no sody,
  so she sent the little boy
    off to the store
      for some sody sallyraytus.
       The little boy
        he went trottin'
         on down the road
         singin',
         "Sody,
          sody,
           sody
          sallyraytus!"

Trotted across the bridge
and on to the store
and got the sody sallyraytus,
and started trottin' on back.

Got to the bridge
and started across,
and an old bear
stuck his head out
from under it, says:

"I'LL EAT YOU UP—
   YOU AND YOUR
      SODY
   SALLYRAYTUS!"

So he swallered the little boy—
him
and his
          sody
            sallyraytus.

The old woman
and the old man
and the little girl
and the pet squirrel
they waited and they waited
for the little boy,
but he didn't come
and didn't come,
so fin'lly the old woman
sent the little girl
after the little boy.
She skipped down the road
and skipped across the bridge
and on to the store,
and the storekeeper told her
the little boy
had already been there
and gone.
So she started

    s k
       i
            n'
       p   i
        p

      back,

and when she got
to the bridge,
the old bear stuck
his head out—

"I EAT A LITTLE BOY,
HIM
AND HIS
SODY
SALLYRAYTUS—
AND I'LL EAT YOU, TOO!"

So he swallered her

    d
    o
    w
    n.

The old woman
and the old man
and the pet squirrel
they waited and waited,
but the little girl
didn't come and didn't come,
so the old woman
sent the old man
after the little boy
and the little girl.
He walked on down the road,
walked across the bridge—
Karump! Karump! Karump!—
and walked on
till he came to the store,
and the storekeeper told him
the little boy
and the little girl
had already been there and gone.

"They must'a stopped somewhere
'side the road to play."

So the old man
he started walkin' on back.
Got to the bridge—

"I EAT A LITTLE BOY,
HIM
AND HIS
SODY
SALLYRAYTUS,
AND I EAT A LITTLE GIRL—
AND I'LL EAT YOU, TOO!"

And the old bear reached
and grabbed the old man
and swallered him.

Well, the old woman
and the pet squirrel
they waited and waited,
but the old man
didn't come and didn't come.
So the old woman
she put out a-hunchety-hunchin'
down the road,
crossed the bridge,
got to the store,
and the storekeeper told her,
"That boy's already
done been here and gone—
him and the little girl
and the old man, too."

So the old woman
she went hunchin' on back—
a-hunchety-hunchety-hunch.
Got to the bridge—

"I EAT A LITTLE BOY,
    HIM
    AND HIS
      SODY
SALLYRAYTUS,
AND I EAT A LITTLE GIRL,
AND I EAT AN OLD MAN—
AND I'LL EAT YOU, TOO!"

Reached out and grabbed her
    and swallered *her*
          u
          p.

Well, the pet squirrel
he waited and he waited
and he waited,
and he went to runnin'
back and forth up there
on the fireboard,
and he was gettin' hungrier
and hungrier;
so fin'lly
he jumped down on the table,
jumped off on the bench,
and jumped to the floor.
Shook his tail out behind him
and out the door
and down the road,
just a-friskin'.
Scuttered across the bridge
and on in the store.
R'ared up on his hindquarters
and looked for the storekeeper,
squarked a time or two,
and when the storekeeper looked
and saw him,
the pet squirrel raised up
on his tiptoes and asked him
had he seen anything
of the little boy
or the little girl
or the old man
or the old woman.

"Law, yes! They all
  done already been here
  and gone.
Surely they ain't *all*
  done stopped 'side the road
  to play."

So the pet squirrel
  he stretched his tail
  out behind him
  and frisked out the door.
Frisked on over the bridge—

"I EAT
A LITTLE BOY,
HIM AND HIS
SODY SALLYRAYTUS,
AND I EAT A LITTLE GIRL,
AND I EAT
AN OLD MAN,
AND I EAT
AN OLD WOMAN—
AND I'LL EAT YOU, TOO!"

The pet squirrel
  he stuck his tail straight up
  in the air and just chittered,
but time the old bear
  made for him,
he was already scratchin'
  halfway up a tree.
The old bear
  he went clamberin' up to get him.
The squirrel got way
  out on a limb,
and the old bear
  started out the limb after him.
The squirrel he jumped
  and caught in the next tree.

"HUMPF!
IF YOU CAN MAKE IT
WITH YOUR LITTLE LEGS,
I *KNOW* I CAN MAKE IT
WITH MY BIG 'UNS!"

And the old bear tried to jump—
didn't quite make it.
Down he went,
and when he hit the ground,
he split

W I D E
O P E N.

The old woman stepped out,
and the old man he stepped out,
and the little girl jumped out,
and the little boy he jumped out.

And the old woman says,
"Where's my sody sallyraytus?"

"Here," says the little boy,
and he handed it to her.

So they went on back
to the house,
and the pet squirrel
he scooted on ahead of 'em,
clumb back up on the fireboard
and curled his tail over his back,
and watched the old woman
till she took the biscuits
out of the oven.
So then
she broke him off a chunk
and blew on it
till it wasn't too hot
and handed it up to him.
And he took it in his forepaws
and turned it over and over
and nibbled on it—
    and when he eat it up,
        he leaned down
        and chittered for some more.
    And he was so hungry
    the old woman
had to hand him chunks
till he'd eat

        TWO
          H
          O
          L
          E

    biscuits.

The Town Mouse
and the Country Mouse

One day the country Mouse invited his friend, the city Mouse, to visit him. The country Mouse put out the best that he had in his pantry— kernels of corn and barley seeds, acorns and nuts, wild berries and sweet-tasting flower stalks. But the town Mouse turned up his nose. "How can you eat such stuff!" he complained. "And how can you live in such a hole! No fun, no excitement, nothing to do from one day to another. Come with me. Let me show you some of the pleasures and sights of the city."

It was a large house to which they came; the country Mouse was struck with its size and splendor. "We will explore it all in the morning," said the town Mouse proudly. "Tonight we will take it easy. Wait until you see the banquet I've made ready for us!"

It was dark when they crept softly into the kitchen. Everyone had gone to bed, but there were still remains of a lavish dinner. There were remnants of cake, bacon rinds, parings of rich cheese, potato peelings, butter to lick, and wine left in the glasses. The country Mouse was in raptures.

Just as they began to enjoy their feast, something terrible descended on them. It was the house cat who sprang with bared teeth and un-sheathed claws through the door. They were lucky to escape into a cranny.

"Good-by," said the country Mouse the next morning. "You have a beautiful house and wonderful food, but I prefer my dried seeds and my quiet hole in the ground."

A crust with comfort is better than a feast with fear.

An Aesop fable adapted by Louis Untermeyer

A RIDDLE

4 DOWN HANG-ERS 4 STIFF STANDERS 2 COAT HOOKS AND 1 DING-DONG

Lettering by Eric Carle

124

HowTwo
went into
Partnership

Story and pictures by Howard P. Pyle

T HIS was the way of it.

Uncle Bear had a pot of honey and a big cheese, but the Great Red Fox had nothing but his wits.

Sensing the story problem.

The fox was for going into partnership, for he says, says he, "A head full of wits is worth more than a pot of honey and a big cheese," which was as true as gospel, only that wits cannot be shared in partnership among folks, like red herring and blue beans, or a pot of honey and a big cheese.

The story problem.

All the same, Uncle Bear was well enough satisfied, and so they went into partnership together, just as the Great Red Fox had said. As for the pot of honey and the big cheese, why, they were put away for a rainy day, and the wits were all that were to be used just now.

"Very well," says the fox, "we'll rattle them up a bit"; and so he did, and this was how.

He was hungry for the honey, was the Great Red Fox. "See, now," said he, "I am sick today, and I will just go and see the Master Doctor over yonder."

Episode 1

But it was not the doctor he went to; no, off he marched to the storehouse, and there he ate part of the honey. After that he lay out in the sun and toasted his skin, for that is pleasant after a great dinner. By and by he went home again.

"Well," says Uncle Bear, "and how do you feel now?"

"Oh, well enough," says the Great Red Fox.

"And was the medicine bitter?" says Uncle Bear.

"Oh, no, it was good enough," says the Great Red Fox.

"And how much did the doctor give you?" says Uncle Bear.

"Oh, about one part of a pot full," says the Red Fox.

Dear, dear! thinks Uncle Bear, that is a great deal of medicine to take, for sure and certain.

Episode 2 Well, things went on as smoothly as though the wheels were greased, until by and by the fox grew hungry for a taste of honey again; and this time he had to go over yonder and see his aunt. Off he went to the storehouse, and there he ate all the honey he wanted, and then, after he had slept a bit in the sun, he went back home again.

"Well," says Uncle Bear, "and did you see your aunt?"

"Oh, yes," says the Great Red Fox, "I saw her."

"And did she give you anything?" says Uncle Bear.

"Oh, yes, she gave me a trifle," says the Great Red Fox.

"And what was it she gave you?" says Uncle Bear.

"Why, she gave me another part of a pot full, that was all," says the Great Red Fox.

"Dear, dear! but that is a queer thing to give," says Uncle Bear.

By and by the Great Red Fox was thinking of honey again, and now it was a christening he had to go to. Off he went to the pot of honey, and this time he finished it all and licked the pot into the bargain.

And had everything gone smoothly at the christening? That was what Uncle Bear wanted to know.

"Oh, smoothly enough," says the Great Red Fox.

"And did they have a christening feast?" says Uncle Bear.

"Oh, yes, they had that," says the Great Red Fox.

"And what did they have?" says Uncle Bear.

"Oh, everything that was in the pot," says the Great Red Fox.

"Dear, dear," says Uncle Bear, "but they must have been a hungry set at the christening."

Well, one day Uncle Bear says, "We'll have a feast and eat up the pot of honey and the big cheese, and we'll ask Father Goat over to help us."

That suited the Great Red Fox well enough, so off he went to the storehouse to fetch the pot of honey and the cheese; as for Uncle Bear he went to ask Father Goat to come and help them eat up the good things.

"See, now," says the Great Red Fox to himself, "the pot of honey and the big cheese belong together, and it is a pity to part them." So down he sat without more ado, and when he got up again, the cheese was all inside of him.

When he came home again there was Father Goat toasting his toes at the fire and waiting for supper; and there was Uncle Bear on the back doorstep sharpening the bread knife.

"Hi!" says the Great Red Fox, "and what are you doing here, Father Goat?"

"I am just waiting for supper, and that is all," says Father Goat.

"And where is Uncle Bear?" says the Great Red Fox.

"He is sharpening the bread knife," says Father Goat.

"Yes," says the Great Red Fox, "and when he is through with that, he is going to cut your tail off."

Dear, dear! but Father Goat was in a great fright; that house was no place for him, and he could see that with one eye shut; off he marched, as though the ground was hot under him. As for the Great Red Fox, he went out to Uncle Bear; "That was a pretty body you asked to take supper with us," says he; "here he has marched off with the pot of honey and the big cheese, and we may sit down and whistle over an empty table between us."

When Uncle Bear heard this, he did not tarry, I can tell you; up he got and off he went after Father Goat. "Stop! stop!" he bawled, "let me have a little at least."

But Father Goat thought that Uncle Bear was speaking of his tail, for he knew nothing of the pot of honey and the big cheese; so he just knuckled down to it, and away he scampered till the gravel flew behind him.

And this was what came of that partnership; nothing was left but the wits that the Great Red Fox had brought into the business; for nobody could blame Father Goat for carrying the wits off with him, and one might guess that without the telling.

Now, as the pot of honey and big cheese were gone, something else must be looked up, for one cannot live on thin air, and that is the truth.

"See, now," says the Great Red Fox, "Farmer John over yonder has a storehouse full of sausages and chitterlings and puddings, and all sort of good things. As nothing else is left of the partnership, we'll just churn our wits a bit and see if we can make butter with them;" that suited Uncle Bear as well as anything he ever heard; so off they marched arm in arm.

By and by they came to Farmer John's house, and no-body was about, which was just what the two rogues wanted; and, yes, there was the storehouse as plain as the nose on your face, only the door was locked. Above was a little window just big enough for the Great Red Fox to creep into, though it was up ever so high. "Just give me a lift up through the window yonder," says he to Uncle Bear, "and I will drop the good things out for you to catch."

So Uncle Bear gave the Great Red Fox a leg up, and—pop!—and there he was in the storehouse like a mouse in the cheese-box. "What shall it be first, sausages or puddings?" he bawled out.

"Hush! hush!" said Uncle Bear.

"Yes, yes," bawled the Red Fox louder than ever, "only tell me which I shall take first, sausages or puddings?"

"Sh-h-h!" said Uncle Bear, "if you are making such a noise as that, you will have them about our ears; take the first that comes and be quick about it."

"Yes, yes," bawled the fox as loud as he was able; "but one is just as handy as another, and you must tell me which I shall take first."

But Uncle Bear got neither pudding nor sausage, for the Great Red Fox had made such a hubbub that Farmer John and his men came running, and three great dogs with them.

"Hi!" said they, "there is Uncle Bear after the sausages and puddings"; and there was nothing for him to do but to lay foot to the ground as fast as he could. All the same, they

caught him over the hill and gave him such a drubbing that
his bones ached for many a long day.

But the Great Red Fox only waited until all the others
were well away on their own business, and then he filled a
bag with the best he could lay his hands on, opened the door
from the inside, and walked out as though it were from his
own barn; for there was nobody to say "No" to him. He hid
the good things away in a place of his own, and it was little
of them that Uncle Bear smelled.

After he had gathered all this, Master Fox came home, groaning as though he had had an awful drubbing; it would have moved a heart of stone to hear him.

"Dear, oh dear! what a drubbing I have had," said he.

"And so have I," said Uncle Bear, grinning over his sore bones as though cold weather were blowing snow in his teeth.

"See, now," said the Great Red Fox, "this is what comes of going into partnership and sharing one's wits with another. If you had made your choice when I asked you, your butter would never have been spoiled in the churning."

That was all the comfort Uncle Bear had, and cold enough it was too. All the same, he is not the first in the world who has lost his dinner and had both the drubbing and the blame into the bargain.

Episode 5 But things do not last forever, and so by and by the good things from Farmer John's storehouse gave out, and the Great Red Fox had nothing in the larder.

"Listen," says he to Uncle Bear, "I saw them shaking the apple trees at Farmer John's today, and if you have a mind to try the wits that belong to us, we'll go and bring a bagful apiece from the storehouse over yonder at the farm."

Yes, that suited Uncle Bear well enough; so off they marched, each of them with an empty bag to fetch back the apples. By and by they came to the storehouse, and nobody was about. This time the door was not locked, so in the both of them went and began filling their bags with apples. The Great Red Fox tumbled them into his bag as fast as ever he could, taking them just as they came, good or bad; but Uncle Bear took his time about it and picked them all over, for since he had come there he was bound to get the best to be had.

So the upshot of the matter was that the Great Red Fox had his bag full before Uncle Bear had picked out half a score of good juicy apples.

"I'll just peep out of the window yonder," says the Great
Red Fox, "and see if Farmer John is coming." But in his sleeve
he said to himself, "I'll slip outside and turn the key of the
door on Uncle Bear, for somebody will have to carry the blame
of this, and his shoulders are broader and his skin tougher than
mine; he will never be able to get out of that little window."
So up he jumped with his bag of apples, to do as he said.

But listen! A hasty man drinks hot broth. And so it was
with the Great Red Fox, for up in the window they had set
a trap to catch rats. Out he jumped from the window—click!
went the trap and caught him by the tail, and there he hung.

"Is Farmer John coming?" bawled Uncle Bear, by and by.

"Hush! hush!" said the Great Red Fox, for he was trying to get his tail out of the trap.

But the boot was on the other leg now. "Yes, yes," bawled Uncle Bear, louder than before, "but tell me, is Farmer John coming?"

"Sh-h-h-h!" says the Great Red Fox.

"No, no," bawled Uncle Bear, as loud as he could, "what I want to know is, is Farmer John coming?"

Yes, he was, for he had heard the hubbub, and here he was with a lot of his men and three great dogs.

"Oh, Farmer John," bawled the Great Red Fox, "don't touch me, I am not the thief. Yonder is Uncle Bear in the pantry, he is the one."

The problem is solved. The story is over. Yes, yes, Farmer John knew how much of that cake to eat; here was the rogue of a fox caught in the trap, and the beating was ready for him. That was the long and the short of it.

When the Great Red Fox heard this, he pulled with all his might and main. Snap! went his tail and broke off close to his body, and away he scampered with Farmer John, the men and the dogs close to his heels. But Uncle Bear filled his bag full of apples, and when all hands had gone racing away after the Great Red Fox, he walked quietly out of the door and off home.

And that is how the Great Red Fox lost his tail in the trap.

What is the meaning of all this? Why, here it is: When a rogue and another crack a nut together, it is not often the rogue who breaks his teeth by trying to eat the hulls. And this too: But when one sets a trap for another, it is a toss of a copper whether or no it flies up and pinches his own fingers.

If there is anything more left in the dish, you may scrape it for yourself.

A Picture for Storytelling

Illustration by Charles Waterhouse

The Swapping Song

verses

1 *My father died but I don't know how;*
he left me a horse to hitch to the plow.

2 *I swapped my horse and got me a cow,*
and in that trade I just learned how.

3 *I swapped my cow and got me a calf,*
and in that trade I lost just half.

4 *I swapped my calf and got me a pig,*
the poor little thing hit never growed big.

5 *I swapped my pig and got me a hen*
to lay me an egg every now and then.

6 *I swapped my hen and got me a cat,*
the pretty little thing by the chimney sat.

7 *I swapped my cat and got me a mouse,*
his tail caught a-fire and he burned down the house.

8 *I swapped my mouse and got me a mole,*
the dad-burned thing went straight down its hole.

A TRADITIONAL FOLKSONG, DESIGNED BY RAY BARBER

To my wing wong waddle! To my Jack Straw Straddle! And Johnny's got his fiddle and he's gone on home!

What Do We Plant When We Plant the Tree?

A POEM BY HENRY ABBEY,
PAINTINGS BY JACK KUNZ AND MEL HUNTER

What do we plant when we plant the tree?
We plant the ship which will cross the sea.
We plant the mast to carry the sails;
We plant the planks to withstand the gales—
The keel, the keelson, the beam, the knee;
We plant the ship when we plant the tree.

What do we plant when we plant the tree?
We plant the houses for you and me.
We plant the rafters, the shingles, the floors;
We plant the studding, the lath, the doors,
The beams and siding, all parts that be;
We plant the house when we plant the tree.

What do we plant when we plant the tree?
A thousand things that we daily see;
We plant the spire that out-towers the crag,
We plant the staff for our country's flag,
We plant the shade, from the hot sun free;
We plant all these when we plant the tree.

Redwoods are among the world's tallest trees. They grow 200 to 300 feet high. The cut wood remains remarkably free from decay caused by weather and insects, and lumbermen prize it for siding on houses, for shingles, and for outdoor furniture.

Eastern white pine was an important lumber tree in Colonial America, but ruthless cutting greatly reduced the supply. Now it is primarily used for knotty pine paneling.

The rubber tree is found all around the world in places within 700 miles of the equator. It needs a hot, wet climate for growing. Its juice, called *latex*, is drained from the tree for making rubber.

Because of its great height and strength, the Douglas fir is the most important timber tree in the world. It is used mainly for lumber and plywood for building, and for telephone poles. It grows exclusively in North America.

The balsam fir tree is used extensively for pulp (for making paper), for wooden boxes and crates, and for a fine clear oil. It is also the most popular of all Christmas trees.

The tall ponderosa pine, second only to Douglas fir as a source of softwood lumber, is used for buildings, railroad ties, telephone poles, posts, and mine timbers.

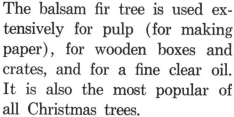

Longleaf pine, sometimes called Georgia pine or yellow pine, is a major source of turpentine. Its lumber is used for constructing homes and railroad boxcars.

The sugar maple tree is perhaps best known as the source of maple syrup. It is also prized for making furniture and hardwood flooring.

White spruce trees are widely used for construction lumber. They also are especially suited for making musical instruments.

The sweet gum tree is named for its sweet, sticky sap. It is an important source of pulp and lumber for furniture.

The white oak tree is a most important source of hardwood lumber. The combination of strength and hardness makes the lumber especially suited for making furniture, ships, and fine buildings.

Lumber from the western hemlock splinters badly and decays rapidly. It is little used for construction, but it is a prime source of pulpwood and tannin, used in tanning leather.

Shagbark hickory, a member of the hardwood walnut family, supplied the spokes for the wheels that crossed the continent and the handles for the axes that cleared the wilderness.

Larch, a European softwood lumber tree, resists decay caused by dampness. For this reason, it is used widely for building in damp, moist, or wet areas. Most of the houses in Venice, Italy, were built on larch pilings.

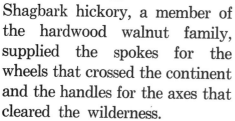

The tall yellow poplar, like the oak, hickory or maple, is another source of hardwood lumber. It is used largely for musical instruments, television cabinets, and other furniture.

Cedar is light, strong, and resistant to decay. It has always been an important lumber tree, particularly to the peoples of the Mediterranean area and to the American Indian.

Mahogany trees in Africa supply most of the mahogany used in the world for furniture, airplane propellers, boats, and decorative beams and flooring in expensive homes and public buildings.

The teak is another very valuable hardwood lumber tree of Africa and Asia. Its large leaves are so rough that natives often use them for sandpaper.

Jak is the famous breadfruit tree. It is the most important hardwood tree in Southeast Asia. Its brilliant yellow wood is especially prized for inlay, cabinets, and furniture.

Although generally unsuited for lumber, palm trees are important economically. They supply coconuts and dates, and their leaves are often used as thatch for covering native huts.

Plugging into MEANINGS

Bill: Hey, Noodles, listen to this.
It's about your relatives.

Noodles: Now, what have they done?

Bill: Well, just listen and you'll find out.
"Nine Little Goblins."

They all climbed up
on a high board-fence,
Nine little goblins
with green-glass eyes.
Nine little goblins that had no sense . . . . .

Noodles: Stop right there, Bill Martin.
This poem is not any good, I think.
Goblins have lots of sense.
They're not dumb.

Bill: . . . . Nine little goblins that had no sense.
And couldn't tell coppers
from cold mince-pies;
And they all climbed up on the fence
and sat—
And I asked them
what they were staring at.

Noodles: This poem is not good, I think.
It's unfair to goblins.

Bill: And they sang: "You're asleep!
There is no board-fence,
And never a goblin
with green-glass eyes!

Noodles: There! Right there!
That poem's all wrong.
Goblins are real
and they have real eyes—not glass eyes.
I know I don't like this poem, Bill Martin.

Bill: 'Tis only a vision the mind invents
After a supper of cold mince-pies,
And you're doomed to dream this way,"
they said—
"*And you sha'n't wake up till you're clean plum dead!*"

Noodles: How can you like that poem, Bill Martin?
I think nobody likes that poem.

Bill: Well, this poem may not be your dish, Noodles.
You probably are so involved defending the goblins
that you didn't hear what the poet was saying.

Noodles: I heard him all right.
He said goblins are dumb.
Say, Bill Martin, who wrote this thing?

Bill: A man named James Whitcomb Riley.

Noodles:

Well, where does he live?

I'm going to go see him right now

and tell him a thing or two about goblins.

Bill:

Well, that's impossible, Noodles.

James Whitcomb Riley is dead.

He's been dead for a long long time.

Noodles:

That's no problem to me, Bill Martin.

I talk to dead people all the time.

Goodbye, Bill.

See you later.

Oodeley, oodeley!

DISAPPEAR
DISAPPEAR
DISAPPEAR
DISAPPEAR

Bill: Isn't it interesting, boys and girls,

what personal meanings Noodles brought to this poem.

This is the way it is with reading:

the author has his meanings,

the reader has his meanings,

and the two of them talk back and forth.

But I'm afraid in this case,

Noodles wasn't talking back and forth.

He blocked the author's meanings out

the moment he heard the author say,

"Nine little goblins that had no sense. . . . ."

From that time on

Noodles was talking to himself.

A good reader listens
both to what the author is saying
and to what he himself is thinking.
He can totally disagree with the author,
just so that he knows what the author says.
The reader can't always confront the author
as Noodles is doing right now,
but the reader develops a bag of know-how
for figuring out the author's meanings.

APPEAR

Noodles: Oh, Bill, you should have been there!
           I like good old James Whitcomb Riley.
           He's a very nice man I think.
           And he wrote a very nice poem.

Bill: Well this is a real switch, Noodles.
           What happened?

Noodles: He wasn't criticizing goblins at all, Bill Martin.
           He was laughing at you people.
           The goblins aren't even real, Bill Martin.
           They're those fake goblins you people see
           when you eat too much.
           So, goodbye, Bill Martin.
           I've got to go now
           and read this poem to my relatives.
           Oodeley, oodeley.

Bill: Well, boys and girls, now I really am stuck in meanings—
           my meanings, the author's meanings, and Noodles'.
           Maybe I *should* go get a piece of cold mince pie.

They went with axe and rifle, when the trail was still to blaze,
They went with wife and children, in the prairie-schooner days,
With banjo and with frying pan—Susanna, don't you cry!
For I'm off to California to get rich out there or die!

WESTERN WAGONS

poem by Stephen Vincent Benét,
paintings by Percy Reeves

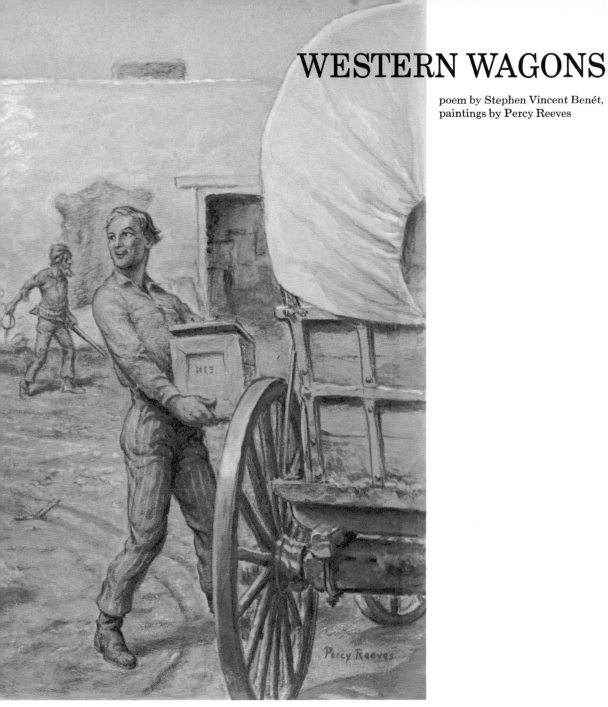

We've broken land and cleared it, but we're tired of where we are.
They say that wild Nebraska is a better place by far.
There's gold in far Wyoming, there's black earth in Ioway,
So pack up the kids and blankets, for we're moving out today!

The cowards never started and the weak died on the road,
And all across the continent the endless campfires glowed.
We'd taken land and settled—but a traveler passed by—
And we're going West tomorrow—Lordy, never ask us why!

We're going West tomorrow, where the promises can't fail.
O'er the hills in legions, boys, and crowd the dusty trail!
We shall starve and freeze and suffer. We shall die, and tame the lands.
But we're going West tomorrow, with our fortune in our hands.

My Mother
Is the Most Beautiful Woman
in the World

A story by Becky Reyher,
pictures by Sylvie Selig

Once upon a time,
long, long ago,
when the harvest season
had come again
in the Ukraine,
the villagers were all busy
cutting and gathering the wheat.
For this is the land
from which most Russians
get the flour for their bread.

Marfa and Ivan
went to the field
early each day,
as did all their children.
There they stayed
until sundown.
Varya was Marfa and Ivan's
youngest little girl.
When everyone went
to the fields in harvest time,
Varya went, too.
Her legs were so short
she had to run and skip
to keep up with her mother's
and father's long steps.

"Varyachka,
  you are a little slow poke!"
her father said to her.
Then, laughing loudly,
he swung her up on his shoulder
where she had to hold tight
to his neck,
for his arms were full
carrying the day's lunch
and the long scythe
to cut the wheat.

In the field,
in the long even rows
between the thick wheat,
Varya knew
just what she must do.
First, she must stay
at least twenty or thirty paces
behind her father,
who now took even greater
and bigger steps,
so that he might have
plenty of room
to swing wide
the newly sharpened scythe.

"Stand back, Varyachka!
Mind the scythe!"
her father warned.
Swish, swish, swish
went his even strokes,
and down came the wheat,
faster and faster,
as he made his great strides.

Soon Marfa began
to follow Ivan.
She gathered the wheat
in sheaves or bunches
just big enough to bind together
with a strand of braided wheat.
Varya, eager to be useful,
helped gather the wheat
and held each bunch
while her mother tied it.
When three sheaves were tied,
they were stacked
against each other
in a little pyramid.

"Careful, Varyachka!"
her mother cautioned,
"the wheat side up!"

After a while,
instead of long rows of wheat,
there were long rows of sheaves,
standing stiffly.

Sometimes
Varya forgot
to follow her mother.
On very hot days
she stopped to rest
upon the warm ground,
and let her tired, bare feet
and toes
tickle the dark, moist earth.

A while later, she ran
and caught up with her mother,
and then her mother
hugged her to her
and wiped her dripping face.
Even though her mother's arms
and bosom were hot and damp,
they felt cool and restful
to Varya.

Day after day,
Ivan, Marfa, and Varya
went to the field,
until all the wheat
was cut and stacked
and none was left growing
in the ground.
Then a big wagon came,
and everyone pitched the wheat
up to the driver
who packed it in solidly
and carefully
and took it
to the threshing barn.
When the harvest was over,
Ivan, Marfa, Varya,
and everyone in the village
prepared for the feast day.
And what a feast they had!

The Russian sun shines
with a warm glow
that makes Russia's wheat
the most nourishing
in the world,
and her fruit and vegetables
the most delicious
that ever grew.
The cherries are the reddest,
largest and juiciest,
the apples the firmest
and crunchiest to the teeth,
the cucumbers
the most plentiful on the vine.
As for the watermelons,
only someone who has seen
a Ukrainian watermelon
really knows
what watermelons should be.

The villagers worked tirelessly
throughout the summer.
Their muscles ached,
but there was a song
in their hearts,
and there were merry chuckles
on their lips.
Hard work produced
a rich harvest.
There would be wheat
for everybody.
It was time, then,
for a grand celebration.

A year ago
Varya was allowed
to share in the excitement
of preparing the feast.
That summer
she helped her mother bake
the little cakes
of plaited flat dough,
stuffed with meat or cabbage.
Piroghki, they were called.
When all the cakes
were rolled out,
Varya's mother said:
"And for you, Varyachka,
a special one, a *piroghochok*."
That meant, in Russian,
a darling little cake.
It also meant
that harvest day was a holiday,
and that Varya's busy mother
could take the time
to bake a special cake for her.

Besides the *piroghki*,
Varya and her mother
brought *blini* to the feast.
These are flat, rolled,
browned, little pancakes,
filled almost to bursting
with jelly or cheese.
They are eaten
smothered with thick cream,
or plain,
held between sticky fingers.

Varya had taken her turn
at rolling out the dough
for the *piroghki*,
for the thinner the dough,
the lighter the *piroghki*.
This is one
of the housewifely lessons
she had to master.
The feast always took place
after church
in the very heart of the village.
Varya came with her parents.
Everybody was there.
The grandmothers,
whom Russians call Baboushka,
and who always wear
a gay kerchief
tied below their chin.
The mothers
with babies in their arms.
The strong,
broad-shouldered fathers.
And the many children,
all with roses in their cheeks.

Tolya, the village leader,
played the accordion.
The minute his music started,
everybody's feet
began to keep time.
The boys whistled
and stamped their feet,
and everybody
clapped their hands.

Men, women, and children
joined in the singing,
as Tolya swung his accordion
into rollicking dance tunes.

The men wore polished,
knee-high, heavy boots,
but they danced
as if their feet were bare.
As the music grew
faster and faster,
their feet grew
lighter and nimbler.
It was as if they
and their partners had wings
that carried them swiftly
by those who were watching.
To Varya it seemed
that the older girls' braids
flew by like birds in the wind.

Tolya stood in the center,
all eyes upon him.
He danced a jigging step or two,
his fingers
never leaving the accordion,
and shouted:
"Too quiet, my friends.
A little more nonsense.
A little more noise.
A few more smiles.
Sing! Sing!
My friends, this is a holiday!
Come! Everyone on their feet!
We must have a dance!"

The girls wore lots of petticoats
under a skirt so wide
you could not tell where it began,
or where it ended.
Around their necks
were many strings of beads
that shone as bright
as a Christmas tree,
all tied with trailing strings
of many colored ribbons.
Some of the little girls
were dressed almost as grandly.
But not Varya, nor most of them.

Varya kept asking her mother:
"When am I going to have
a beautiful dance costume
with lots of beads?"

And Varya's mother would say:
"When you are
a grown-up young lady, Varya."

Always it seemed to Varya
she just could not wait
until she was grown-up.

Varya was an impatient little girl.
Her impatience
was like a teasing toothache.
Today it was so great
she felt choked,
as if she had swallowed
a whole watermelon.

For today was the last day
for gathering the wheat.
By evening
all the wheat would be cut,
stacked in pyramids,
and waiting for the wagon
to take it
to the threshing barn.
Tomorrow
another wonderful feast day
and celebration
would come around again.
Varya could hardly wait
for the feast day to begin.

Bright and early
Marfa, Ivan, and Varya
went to the wheat field.
"We must get to it,"
warned Ivan,
"This is our last day
to get the wheat in!"

"It has been a good crop, Ivan,
hasn't it?" asked Marfa.

"Indeed, yes!"
Ivan answered heartily,
"and it will mean
a good warm winter
with plenty to eat.
We have much to be thankful for."

Marfa and Ivan worked
quicker and harder than ever.
They did not seem
to notice the hot sun.
The wheat swished
almost savagely
as it came rushing down.

But to Varya
the day seemed the longest
she had ever lived.
The sun seemed hotter
than on any other day,
and her feet
seemed almost too heavy to lift.

Varya peered
into the next row of wheat
which was not yet cut.
There it was cool and pleasant,
and the sun did not bear down
with its almost unbearable heat.
Varya moved in
just a little further
to surround herself
with that blessed coolness.
"How lucky I am!" she thought,
"to be able to hide
away from the hot sun.
I will do this
for just a few minutes.
Surely Mamochka will not mind
if I do not help her
all the day."

Soon Varya grew sleepy,
for in so cool a place,
one could curl up
and be very quiet
and comfortable.

Varya called,
"Mama," "Mama," "Mamochka,"
but there was no answer.

Sometimes
her mother got ahead of her
and was so busy with her work
she did not hear.

When Varya woke,
she jumped to her feet
and started to run
toward her mother.
But her mother
was nowhere in sight.

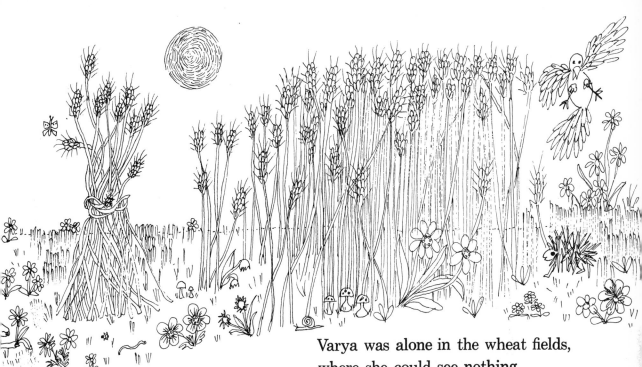

Varya was alone in the wheat fields,
where she could see nothing
but tall pyramids of wheat
towering above her.
When she called out,
her voice brought no response,
no help.
Overhead the sun was not so bright
as it had been.
Varya knew that soon
it would be night
and that she must find her mother.

"Maybe if I run along the row,
I will catch up with her,"
Varya thought.
She ran and ran,
and soon she was out of breath,
but nowhere
could she see her mother.

"Maybe I have gone
in the wrong direction,"
she said to herself.
So she ran the other way.
But here, too,
there was no trace of her mother.

Varya cut through the last
of the wheat
that had not yet been cut,
breaking her own pathway,
which bent and hurt the wheat.
She would not have done this,
had she not been frightened.

When it was almost dark,
Varya tumbled into a clearing
where several men and women
had paused to gossip
after the day's work.
It took her only a second
to see that these were strangers
and that neither her mother
nor father were among them.

The little girl stared
ahead of her,
not knowing what to do.
One of the men spied her
and said in a booming voice
which he thought was friendly,
"Look what we have here!"

Everyone turned to Varya.
She was sorry that
with so many strangers
looking at her
she had her hair caught back
in a tiny braid
with a bit of string
and that she was wearing
only her oldest,
most faded dress.
Surely, too, by now
her face and hands must be
as streaked with dirt
as were her legs and dress.
This made her burst into tears.

"Poor little thing,"
cried one of the women,
putting her arms around Varya.
"She is lost!"
But this sympathy
and the strange voices
made Varya want her mother
all the more.
She could not help crying.

"We must know her name,
and the name of her mother
and father.
Then we can unite them,"
said the women.

"Little girl, little girl,"
  they said.
"What is your name?
  What is your mother's
  and father's name?"
But Varya was too unhappy
  to speak.
Finally, because her longing
  for her mother was so great,
  she sobbed out:
*"My mother
  is the most beautiful woman
  in the world!"*

All the men and women smiled.
The tallest man, Kolya,
  clapped his hands
  and laughingly said,
"Now we have something to go on."

This was long, long ago,
  when there were no telephones
  and no automobiles.
If people wanted
  to see each other
  or carry a message,
  they went on their two feet.

From every direction,
  friendly, good-hearted boys
  ran to village homes
  with orders to bring back
  the beautiful women.

"Bring Katya, Manya,
  Vyera, Nadya,"
  the tall man, Kolya,
  called to one boy.
"Ay, but don't forget
  the beauty, Lisa,"
  he called to still another boy.

The women came running.
There were orders from Kolya,
  the village leader.
Also the mothers
  who had left the fields early
  to get supper for their families
  thought perhaps this was indeed
  their child who was lost.

As each beautiful woman
  came rushing up,
  blushing and proud
  that she had been chosen,
  Kolya would say to her:
"We have a little lost one here.
  Stand back, everyone,
  while the little one tells us
  if this is her mother!"

The mothers laughed and pushed,
  and called to Kolya:
"You big tease!
  What about asking each mother
  if this is her child?
  We know our children!"

To Varya this was very serious,
for she was lost
and she was desperate
without her mother.
As she looked
at each strange woman,
Varya shook her head
in disappointment
and sobbed harder.
Soon every beauty
from far and near,
from distances much further
than a child could have strayed,
had come and gone.
Not one of them
was Varya's mother.

The villagers were really worried.
They shook their heads.
Kolya spoke for them.
"One of us will have to take
the little one home
for the night.
Tomorrow may bring
fresh wisdom to guide us!"

Just then
a breathless, excited woman
came puffing up to the crowd.
Her face was big and broad,
and her body even larger.

Her eyes were little pale slits
between a great lump of a nose.
The mouth was almost toothless.
Even as a young girl
everyone had said,
"A homely girl like Marfa
is lucky to get a good husband
like Ivan."

"Varyachka!" cried the woman.

"Mamochka!" cried the little girl,
and they fell
into each other's arms.
The two of them
beamed upon each other.
Varya cuddled into that ample
and familiar bosom.
The smile Varya had longed for
was once again shining upon her.

All of the villagers
smiled thankfully
when Varya looked up
from her mother's shoulder
and said with joy:
"This is my mother!
I told you my mother
is the most beautiful woman
in the world!"

The group of friends
and neighbors, too,
beamed upon each other,
as Kolya repeated the proverb
so well known to them,

a proverb which little Varya
had just proved:
*"We do not love people
because they are beautiful,
but they seem beautiful to us
because we love them."*

PAINTING BY MURIEL WOOD

Unapproachable

Getting to know you
Is like taking a long walk
To my home next door.
So close, and yet
Between us lie
Side streets and alleys.
(I'm getting lost.)
I cannot ask directions
For who knows the way?
                              Only you!

A POEM BY AGNES PRATT

The Writers' Reader HONORS COLLECTION:
1962-1966 INSTITUTE OF AMERICAN INDIAN ARTS
SANTA FE, NEW MEXICO

PART II

RESPONDING
TO READING

Noodles: Oodeley, oodeley!
Here I come, Bill Martin,
full of response-ability.

Bill: Hello, Noodles.
I see you've already noticed
we're starting the second half of the book—
Responding to Reading.

Noodles: Oh, I've been reading this part
for a long long time.
I didn't tell you all this, did I?
I sneaked ahead.

Bill: That's all right, Noodles.
I hope the boys and girls and teachers and everybody
know that you can skip around in this book
from front to back to middle to in-between
any time you like.

168

Noodles: That's what I like...
skipping around and around and around,
reading here, reading there,
reading reading everywhere.
Sometimes I see things and I just can't wait.
I have to look at it right that very minute.

Bill: Now we're going to think of ways
to respond to what we read, Noodles.
Reading has to be for something
besides just recognizing words.

Noodles: Like having a real whole lot of fun.
Don't you like to have fun, Bill Martin?
I like to laugh when I read sometimes.
And I'm going to tell you something else,
but don't you tell anybody.
Do you promise?

Bill: I promise.

Noodles: Then I'll whisper it in your ear.

Bill: Just say it out loud, Noodles.
Nobody is here to hear you.

Noodles: That's not the way you do with a secret.
You don't tell the whole wide world.
I'm going to whisper in your nice little ear.

Bill: Alright, whisper it then.

Noodles: Which ear do you want me to tell it in, Bill,
the one right here
or the one on the other side of your little head?

Bill: Take your choice, Noodles.

Noodles: I think I like this one.
It's cleaner.
Pss...pss...pss...pss...pss...pss...pss...
pss...pss...pss...pss...pss...pss...pss!

Bill: I never knew you ever cried, Noodles.

Noodles: Sometimes I do when the story is sad,
but I don't let anybody see me.

Bill: Well, I cry too
when the story is sad, Noodles.
Many people do.
"The Steadfast Tin Soldier" is the story of a brave man
but it makes me cry every time I read it.
There's nothing wrong with shedding tears.
That's one way to respond to reading.

Noodles: I'll betcha an astronaut wouldn't cry,
I'll betcha.
He's too brave.

Bill: That isn't true, Noodles.
You're not a sissy just because you cry.
Crying is part of being a human being.
Sometimes we cry because we're sad,
sometimes because we're glad.

Noodles: Cry when you're glad?
I never did it that way.

Bill: Why, Noodles, I've seen football players
cry with joy because they won a game.
I've seen people cry with joy
because they're glad to be back together again.
I've seen people laugh until they cried.

Noodles: I know one time I almost cried, Bill Martin.
That was when you were reading about those goblins.
I was just so very very mad,
I was sad.

Bill: Anger is another way of responding to reading.
And there are many other ways
which we will be discussing
in this part of the book:
storytelling,
reading aloud,
choral reading,
creative dramatics,
wondering about words,
choosing what you like and don't like,
and finding out more than the story told you.

Noodles: Girls and boys and ba-bees,
teachers and principals and parents,
protect your ears!
Bill Martin is making another speech.
I don't know what you boys and girls are going to do,
but I'm really getting out of here right now.
Goodbye, everybody!
Oodeley, oodeley!

Bill: Well, that's another way
to respond to reading, boys and girls.
You can always walk out on the author
by closing the book.

The hills are alive
    with the sound of music,
With songs they have sung
    for a thousand years.
The hills fill my heart
    with the sound of music.
My heart wants to sing
    every song it hears.

My heart wants to beat
    like the wings of the birds
    that rise from the lake
    to the trees.
My heart wants to sigh
    like a chime
    that flies from a church
    on a breeze.

I go to the hills
    when my heart is lonely,
I know I will hear
    what I've heard before.
My heart will be blessed
    with the sound of music
And I'll sing...
    once more.

the sound of music

A song by Richard Rodgers
and Oscar Hammerstein II,
photograph by Bill Ratcliffe

173

Ever since the birth
of the twin heifers,
Cow had felt herself superior.
She had felt that even giving
the usual amount of milk
was not necessary.
Her picture,
together with that
of her twin daughters
had been in the Hillsborough *News*
with a printed piece
about them.
Cow had decided that
now her time had come
for a life of pleasure.
As Cow would have put it,
she could *rest on her laurels.*
And this, in fact, was
just what Cow
had been doing that day,
resting among laurel bushes
and stuffing herself
with windfall apples
where a pile of them

COW

Story by Carolyn Sherwin Bailey,
illustrated with lithographs by Ruth Gannett

*This description of a proud cow who
ate too many rotten apples is humorous
writing at its best. As you read it aloud,
you will discover that the rhythm of
the sentences jigs right along with Cow
as she waddles home.*

had been dumped
under the lee
of Temple Mountain.
But first,
as she had started out
on her adventure
that morning,
Cow had stopped
in the truck garden
and eaten
a whole winter squash.
It was an acorn squash,
with a hard green shell
and richly yellow inside.
She had eaten
the acorn squash,
shell and all.
Then,
on a morning breeze,
Cow had got a whiff
of the rotting apples.
It had been
beyond her power to resist.
When she had eaten
more of the apples
than was wise,
Cow had arisen
with difficulty
from her bed of laurels,
staggered down to the road
and started home.

Cow had lost all sense of respectability.
She was not walking, but jigging her way home,
doing a poor kind of tap dance
from one side of the road to the other,
past the meadow,
by the mowing field,
trying at last to get through the barnyard gate.
She felt that it had been a successful day.
As she came capering along,
Cow gave deep-throated *moo*'s of satisfaction.
She made it between the gateposts,
but inside the barn she collapsed.
As happens often when one eats too much,
Cow had a tremendous stomach ache.
Her *moo*'s changed from hilarity to calls for help.

The farmer started toward the barn
with a bottle of medicine.
If Cow had been able to swallow
in a civilized way like the horses and the sheep,
her medicine would have gone down easily.
But since Cow ordinarily lived on cuds,
chewing them for long periods of time,
and had a special digestive system,
she swallowed differently from most animals.
She had to be stood on her back legs
against the side of her stall,
which was an uncomfortable and undignified stance,
to have a dose of medicine poured down her throat.

Bedtime found her
in the soft straw of the stall,
and the crooning of the hens on their perches
sang her to sleep.

Dust
of Snow

The way a crow
Shook down on me
The dust of snow
From a hemlock tree

Has given my heart
A change of mood
And saved some part
Of a day I had rued.

BY ROBERT FROST

Sunning

Old Dog lay in the summer sun
Much too lazy to rise and run.
He flapped an ear
At a buzzing fly.
He winked a half opened
Sleepy eye.
He scratched himself
On an itching spot,
As he dozed on the porch
Where the sun was hot.
He whimpered a bit
From force of habit
While he lazily dreamed
Of chasing a rabbit.
But Old Dog happily lay in the sun
Much too lazy to rise and run.

BY JAMES S. TIPPETT

The Cowboy Today

Gerald McCann is both an artist and a Texas cowboy. Therefore, it's natural that his favorite subjects for painting are cowboys and horses. Here are seven of his water color paintings that make clear statements about the life of a modern cowboy.

It's a peaceful day. A cowboy "takes it easy in the saddle" as cattle are driven from one pasture to another where grass is more plentiful. The cattle are being fattened for marketing.

Old Pete, the pack horse, is being given a drink after a long trip from another part of the ranch. He carries supplies for a wrangler who is "camping out" to mend fences.

This bucking Apache is being broken to ride. He's a young horse. The feel of a cowboy on his back is a new, frightening experience. He bucks wildly, snorts and rears, but the cowboy probably will best him.

Top of the Morning is an older horse. He's been ridden enough to know every trick of throwing a cowboy out of the saddle. Notice how much more of a twist is in his bucking than in the horse's above. Since the cowboy has his lariat, he obviously was preparing to go to work and didn't expect the horse to buck. What he didn't know was that one of his "buddies" had put a burr under the saddle in the hope that he would get "throwed."

A wrangler is hired to ride the range looking for cows that have strayed, to round up livestock for shipping to market, and for going on cattle drives to brand calves.

The wrangler has spotted a calf that has been separated from its mother. He'll carry it back in his saddle, if necessary, to return it to the fold.

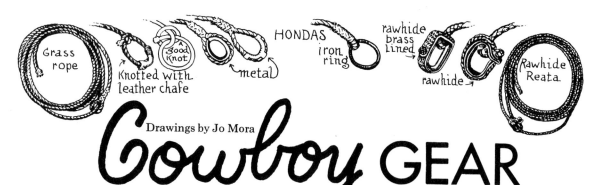

Grass rope

Knotted with leather chafe

metal

HONDAS

iron ring

rawhide brass lined

rawhide

Rawhide Reata

Good Knot

Drawings by Jo Mora

Cowboy GEAR

Here's an article for picture reading.

Have you ever stopped to think about how many times you read pictures instead of words? Picture-reading is one of the most important reading skills. These pages invite picture-reading. The drawings are by Jo Mora, and even though you haven't had experience with the particular kinds of cowboy gear and even if you can't pronounce the words, you'll probably find yourself getting meanings from the pictures and enjoying the whole experience.

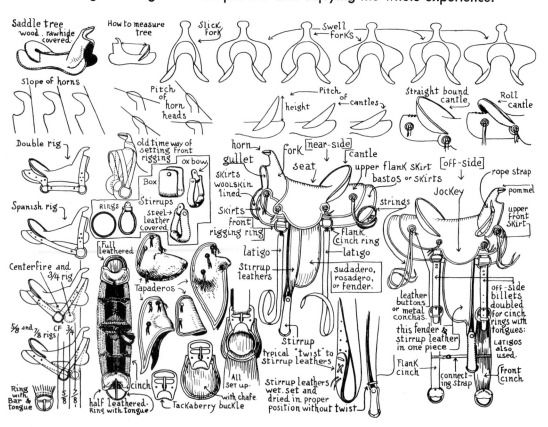

Saddle tree wood . rawhide covered.

Slope of horns

How to measure tree

Slick fork

Swell forks

Pitch of horn heads

Pitch of cantles

height

Straight bound cantle

Roll cantle

Double rig

old time way of setting front rigging

ox bow

Box

horn gullet

fork

near-side

cantle

upper flank skirt

off-side

rope strap

Skirts woolskin lined

seat

bastos or skirts

pommel

Spanish rig

Rings

Stirrups

steel leather covered

Skirts front rigging ring

strings

Jockey

upper front skirt

Full leathered

latigo

flank cinch ring

latigo

Centerfire and 3/4 rig

Tapaderos

Stirrup leathers

sudadero, rosadero, or fender.

leather buttons or metal conchas.

off-side billets doubled for cinch rings with tongues:

5/8 and 7/8 rigs

CF 3/4

this fender & stirrup leather in one piece

Latigos also used.

Stirrup

typical "twist" to stirrup leathers

Flank cinch

Front cinch

Ring with Bar & tongue

5/8 7/8

half leathered. Ring with tongue

cinch

All set up. with chafe

Tackaberry buckle

Stirrup leathers wet, set and dried in proper position without twist

connecting strap

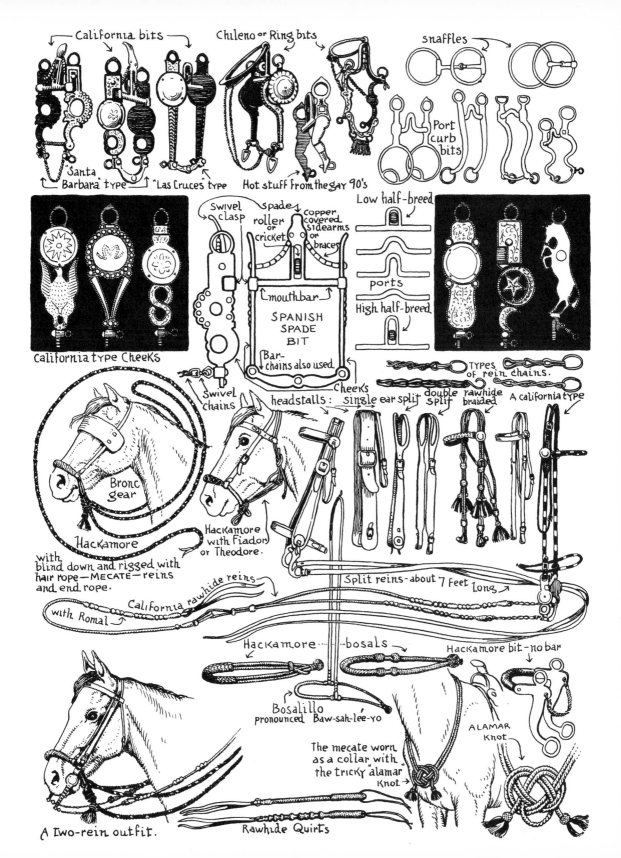

California bits

Chileno or Ring bits

snaffles

"Santa Barbara" type

"Las Cruces" type

Hot stuff from the gay 90's

Port curb bits

California type Cheeks

Swivel clasp

spade roller or cricket

copper covered sidearms or braces

Low half-breed

ports

High half-breed

mouthbar

SPANISH SPADE BIT

Bar-chains also used

Swivel chains

Cheeks headstalls: single ear split — double split — rawhide braided — A california type

Types of rein chains.

Swivel chains

Bronc gear

Hackamore

with blind down and rigged with hair rope—MECATE—reins and end rope.

Hackamore with Fiador or Theodore.

Split reins-about 7 feet long

California rawhide reins

with Romal

Hackamore — bosals — Hackamore bit—no bar

Bosalillo
pronounced Baw-sah-lee-yo

The mecate worn as a collar with the tricky "alamar" knot

ALAMAR Knot

A two-rein outfit.

Rawhide Quirts

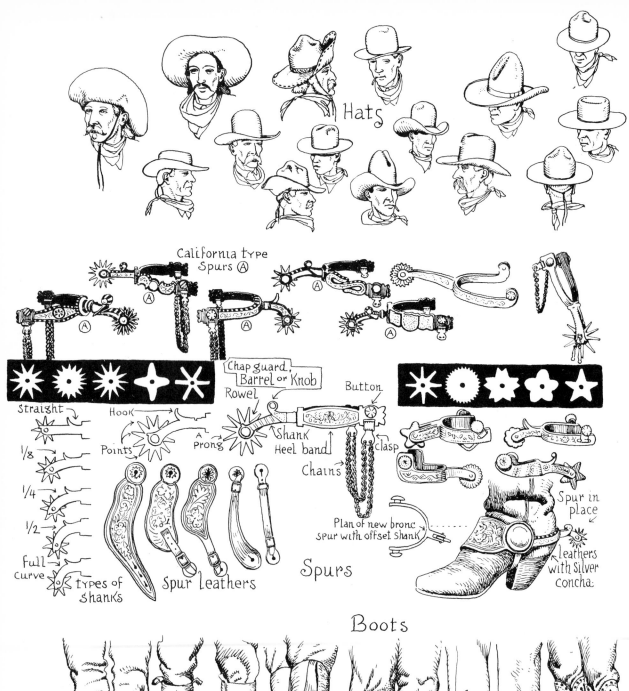

Hats

California type
Spurs (A)

Chap guard,
Barrel or Knob
Rowel
Button
Points
A Prong
Shank
Heel band
Clasp
Chains

Hook

straight
1/8
1/4
1/2
Full
curve
types of
shanks

Spur Leathers

Plan of new bronc
spur with offset shank

Spurs

Spur in
place

Leathers
with silver
concha

Boots

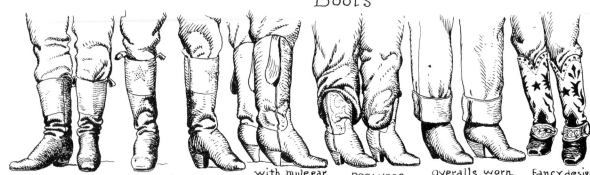

from the '70's   Turn of the Century   with mule ear straps   pee wees   overalls worn over boots   fancy designs and colors.

Home On the Range

Oh, give me a home
where the buffalo roam,
where the deer and the antelope play,
where seldom is heard
a discouraging word,
and the skies are not cloudy all day.

The Red Man was pressed
from his home in the West,
he is likely no more to return
to the banks of Red River,
where seldom if ever
his flickering campfires burn.

Astraddle

If a feller been astraddle
Since he's big enough to ride,
And has had to sling his saddle
On most any colored hide,
Though it's nothing they take pride in,
Still most fellers I have knowed,
If they ever done much ridin',
Have at different times been throwed.

ANONYMOUS

185

A Fox Story

A story by Allen Sollers,
pictures by William Reusswig

This is a true story.
It began one noontime when I was a boy
in a country school in Calvert County, Maryland.
There were sixteen of us in school, ranging from first to eighth graders.

We were on the playground at noon,
when Charles suddenly stopped and held up his hands for silence.
He cocked his head to one side, listening.
Then he asked, "Do you hear that? Them's hounds!"
There was no mistaking the sound of hounds on the trail of a fox.

Each of us had heard this familiar sound most of our lives,
because fox hunting was a favorite sport in Calvert County.

"I'll bet they're coming this way," Charles said breathlessly.

"The last time they chased that fox,
he crossed through the cornfield
and ran right down to Rawlings Cove," I said.
Capt'n Jim, who never missed a hunt if he could help it,
had told me about the last one
when the fox had outsmarted the hounds
along the north shore of the cove.

"Let's go!" Henry shouted.
"Maybe the fox is headed for the cove again!"

"It sounds like it!" exclaimed Charles.

187

Charles took off across the schoolyard.
The rest of us upper-grade boys followed.

"What about us?" the girls shouted.

"We'll tell you all about it when we get back!"
Charles answered.

Charles and Henry led the way through the woods
to the fence that bordered the lower end of the cornfield.
When we arrived at the fence,
the pack of hounds was coming closer.

"If Capt'n Jim finds us here, he'll skin us alive," I said.
"He has no use for kids on a fox hunt."

Charles turned quickly to climb a huge pine tree.
The rest of us followed up the stair-step limbs
and climbed quickly to the tree-top.
There we settled down in our majestic grandstand
to wait for whatever might happen.

Then, heavenly days!
A full-grown red fox trotted out of the bushes
just to the left of us
and stopped at the edge of the field,
looking in the direction of the hounds.

Fortunately, the wind was in our favor.
The fox obviously had not caught our scent.
He stood calmly, unalarmed by the approach of the dogs.

His actions were puzzling.
It looked as if he were waiting for the hounds
instead of running from them.
His unruffled coat and his brisk step
showed no signs of weariness.
I knew that we were seeing a fox
use all of his cunning to avoid the dogs,
but just what he was up to baffled me.

A moment later we were even more confused.
A second fox appeared at the edge of the cornfield.
This fox was much smaller than the first,
and was apparently the vixen mate of the first fox.
There was no doubt that this second fox
was the one the hounds were trailing.

Coming along the edge of the cornfield,
the vixen ran directly to her mate.
She brushed against him,
and then ran to a gap in the fence
that surrounded the field.
She leaped to the top rail of the log fence and,
like a tightrope walker,
moved quickly along until she vanished from sight.

In spite of the fact that the pack of dogs was coming quite close,
the male fox showed no alarm.
With calm deliberateness,
he flattened down on his stomach
and began crawling on the grass.

He continued moving in this fashion toward the fence
where his mate had leaped from the ground to the top rail.
After he had passed five or six feet beyond this point,
he leaped to his feet and flashed away toward the cove.

All of us had heard that foxes
would relieve each other when they
were being chased by hounds.
Here we had seen it happen!
The male fox had come to the rescue of his mate
and was deliberately leading the dogs in another direction!
We were greatly impressed
by the way in which the fox had made sure
that the hounds would follow him
instead of his tired mate.

Suddenly, the pack of hounds
burst out of the woods with frenzied baying.
They followed the scent of the fox
along the edge of the cornfield
and to the gap in the fence.
In a few moments, they had passed beneath us
and were off chasing the male fox to the cove.
Not one of them caught the scent of the vixen
that had escaped them by running along the top of the rail fence.

The hunters arrived quickly, following the dogs.
They passed below us without knowing
that we had viewed them from our treetop seats.
When we were certain that they were gone,
we scrambled down the tree in wild amazement.

On Saturday six of us boys who had our mothers' consent
gathered at Charles' house for another day "in the woods."
What we didn't tell our mothers or anybody else
was that we were going to spy on Capt'n Jim and the men
on another fox hunt.

The men were so mad that the fox had outsmarted them
that they had set Saturday for another try.
The best thing we boys could hope for
was another look at the foxes.
Naturally we assumed the hunt would lead to the cove
where we had hidden before.

It was almost eleven o'clock when we arrived at the cove
and climbed up a big tree on the south side of the water.
We agreed that no one would call out or say anything,
no matter what happened.

"We'll catch thunder if Capt'n Jim
finds us spying on him," I said.

"He won't find us," Charles said.
"We'll be careful."

Each of us had brought a couple of apples
which we slipped out of our pockets
and began eating as silently as we could.

Our timing was excellent!
Shortly after we were settled in the treetop,
we heard the hounds trailing the fox.
Their baying steadily became louder.
Charles gave a signal
for all of us to remain perfectly still,
and pointed to the opposite side of the cove
where the fox might first appear.

Our tension mounted as we watched intently
for the first sign of the fox.
The baying of the hounds indicated
that he was coming closer all the time.

Suddenly, the fox broke from the bushes at a dead run!
He crossed the clearing between the bushes
and the shore in a flash.

When he reached the edge of the water,
he made a tremendous leap into the creek!
It looked to me as if the fox
had jumped at least twenty feet!
Charles said later that he was sure
the leap had been longer than that.

In any event, when the fox hit the water,
he began to swim up the cove and out from the shore.
We thought he was swimming around a fallen, giant pine tree
whose thick, downward limbs held the trunk
a few feet above the water.
The fox, however, had a different idea.

When he reached the outer end of the tree,
he turned and swam in among its branches.
He moved in close under the tree trunk,
then disappeared from sight.
Obviously, he had flattened himself
against one of the big limbs,
with only the tip of his nose above the water.
In this position, he would be most difficult for the hounds to find.

Soon the hunters
arrived. There was
The hounds broke into
eagerly sniffed the scent
water's edge. Then they lost
men moved up and down the
the track or scent of the fox.
trace of their quarry did they

and the hounds
a great commotion.
the clearing, and
of the fox up to the
it. Both dogs and
shore, seeking
But not a
find.

195

Then Capt'n Jim's most dependable hound, Old Belle,
jumped upon the trunk of the fallen tree
and began to follow it out from the shore.

"Oh, go back, old hound, go back!"
was my silent prayer.
I was sure that my companions felt the same as I did.

The hound was now halfway out to the end of the tree trunk!
My blood pounded in my veins
as I contemplated the fate of the fox.
Was the fox holding his breath as I was?
Could Old Belle see the fox submerged in the water?
Could she possibly smell the fox's breath at that distance?

Would the hound work her way out to the end of the tree trunk,
or would the protruding limbs stop her?

As if in answer to our prayers,
the hound stopped.
She slowly turned around and started back toward the shore.

Momentarily, the fox seemed safe.
Then a hunter asked,
"Do you suppose the fox is out on that old tree?"

"No," replied Capt'n Jim.
"That was my best hound.
Old Belle would have spotted that fox
if he was in the vicinity of that tree.
I think that fox swam the creek."

196

"I'll take my hounds
around the head of the cove
    and down the other shore.
    You fellows follow
    this shoreline down,
    and one of us should find
    the spot where the fox
    left the water
to go back in the woods."

Once again I prayed,
    "Oh, Fox,
    don't move too soon!"

Capt'n Jim
    and his hounds
    were coming around
        the head of the cove.

Capt'n Jim and his hounds
passed below us without a moment's hesitation.
Each party had examined the shoreline
without finding a trace of the fox.

"That scamp got away again," Capt'n Jim called to his friends.
"I think he followed the swamp up toward Murray's farm.
Take the road on your side
and meet me at the schoolhouse."

Then they were gone.
Minutes passed before the fox moved.
Finally, we noticed a slight ripple in the water
where the fox had hidden.
He raised his head above the surface.
He made no sound.
When he was sure that he was safe,
he swam back down the cove
to the spot where he had entered the water.
He crawled up on a flat rock
that lay quite close to the shore,
and shook the water from his fur.

After looking cautiously about,
He leapt from the rock to the grass
and was gone.

Then Charles gave the signal
to break silence.
We all started chattering at once.
We climbed down the tree,
elated by the fox's cunning.

"That's the smartest fox I ever knew,"
said Henry.

"And we won't ever tell his secret," said Charles.
"Let's all pledge that we won't tell his hiding place."

As far as I know,
not one of us boys ever broke the pledge in the fox's lifetime.

Frogs and Kites

A POEM BY SUSAN OLESZKOWICZ

Frogs fly and kites jump.
No, I mean frogs jump and *fly kites!*
No, that's wrong.
But now I know what I mean,
Frogs *flump* and kites *jy!*

The Concrete Mixer

Sand, shovel and shingle
Mortar,
Round mouth rattling,
Always being fed,
Always turning,
Spits out food,
Forever hungry.
Powerful,
Noisy,
A useful tool,
Three teeth.
Stark and ugly,
Silent
At day's end.

Timothy Langley
AGE 11
NEW ZEALAND

FROM "MIRACLES" BY RICHARD LEWIS
SIMON AND SCHUSTER © 1966 BY RICHARD LEWIS

The Frog
on the Log

POEM BY ILO ORLEANS,
ART BY ERIC CARLE

There once was a green
  Little frog, frog, frog,
Who played in the wood
  On a log, log, log!

A screech owl sitting
  In a tree, tree, tree,
Came after the frog
  With a scree, scree, scree!

When the frog heard the owl
  In a flash, flash, flash,
He leaped in the pond
  With a splash, splash, splash!

READING ALOUD AND STORYTELLING

APPEAR
APPEAR
APPEAR
APPEAR
APPEAR

Noodles: Oh, hello, Bill Martin,
but don't say nothin' to me
'cause I'm busy reading.

Bill: Reading what?

Noodles: Soup.

Bill: Reading what?

Noodles: Beautiful soup!
Do you want some?

Bill: No, but I'd like to hear about it.

Noodles: I was hoping you'd ask me to do that, Bill.
Put on your napkin
and get out of my way, Bill,
'cause here comes the soup!

Bill: Is it chicken-noodle?

Noodles: NOOOOOODLES!
How can you say that?
You're not making soup out of me!

Bill: Oh, come on, Noodles.
No one wants a ghost in his soup.

Noodles: I don't think you have ever tried
a ghost in your soup, Bill Martin.
A ghost might be a very very tasty treat.
Come to think of it,
I eat ghost soup all the time at my house.

Bill: Well, get on with the reading, Noodles.
I'm waiting for that beautiful soup.

Beautiful Soup
by
Lewis Carroll

Beautiful Soup, so rich and green,
Waiting in a hot tureen!
Who for such dainties would not stoop?
Soup of the evening, beautiful Soup!

Soup of the evening, beautiful Soup!
Beau-ootiful Soo-oop!
Beau-ootiful Soo-oop!
Soo-oop of the e-e-evening,
Beautiful, beautiful Soup!

Beautiful Soup! Who cares for fish,
Game, or any other dish?
Who would not give all else for two
Pennyworth only of beautiful Soup?
Pennyworth only of beautiful Soup?
Beau-ootiful Soo-oop!
Beau-ootiful Soo-oop!
Soo-oop of the e-e-evening,
Beautiful, beauti-FUL SOUP!

Bill: Bravo! Bravo!
You read that well, Noodles!

Noodles: Yes, I did read that very very well, Bill Martin.
That is one of my most favorite stories
because I really do like soup.

Bill: Well, here's a soup story, Noodles,
I can tell you.
I remember it from my childhood,
when my grandmother used to tell stories
while she was ironing shirts
or getting a meal on the table.
She was a great storyteller,
telling the stories in a simple natural way,
just as if she were talking
about the coming and going of the weather.

Sometimes I sway like a tree and whisper.

Once upon a time there was an old woodcutter and his wife
who lived at the edge of a road going through the woods.
They were very poor with little in their pantry,
but they took all of their vegetables and a little piece of ham
and made a kettle of soup, just enough for three.
Then they invited the Lord to supper,
and he sent word that he would come that night.

Along about suppertime,
an old beggar came to the door
and asked
for something to eat.
The old woman thought,
"I'll let him have
my part of the soup.
He needs it worse than I do."
So she fed the beggar and he thanked her and left.

Sometimes I CHANT!

Before long a little ragged boy came knocking on the door.
He looked so cold and starved that the old folks took him in.

And the old man thought, "I'll let him have
   my part of the soup.
   I'm not much hungry."
   So he fed the boy and let him sit and get warm.
The old lady asked the boy to stay the night
but he said he couldn't and thanked them and left.

   By and by the old man and the old woman
      saw the Lord coming.
      They met him at the gate and said,
      "We've waited so long!
      We were afraid you had forgotten to come."
   "No," said the Lord, "I didn't forget.
   I've been here twice already."

   And from that day onwards,
   the old man and his wife
   always found the kettle full of soup
   no matter how much or how often they ate.

Noodles: Oh, I do like that story very very much.
         It makes me feel so good.

Bill: I like it, too, Noodles.

Noodles: Bill Martin, did I hear you
         invite me to your house for soup tonight?

Bill: Well . . . yes, Noodles.
       It'll be beef-noodle.

Noodles: Oh, I did just remember,
         I can't come tonight I think.
         Goodbye, Bill.
         Oodeley, oodeley.

Sing! every bird on every bough—
  Sing! every living, loving thing—
Sing any song, and anyhow,
  But Sing! Sing! Sing!

BY JAMES WHITCOMB RILEY

Hot weather? Yes; but really not,
Compared with weather twice as hot.
Find comfort, then, in arguing thus,
And you'll pull through victorious!—
For instance, while you gasp and pant
And try to cool yourself—and can't—
With soda, cream and lemonade,
The heat at ninety in the shade,—
Just calmly sit and ponder o'er
These same degrees, with ninety more
On top of them, and so concede
The weather now is cool indeed!

BY JAMES WHITCOMB RILEY

The Seasons

Pictures by Jerome Snyder, American Artists Group

Sing hey! Sing hey!
For Christmas Day
Twine mistletoe and holly
For friendship glows
In winter snows,
And so let's all be jolly.

AN OLD RHYME

A wee little worm in a hickory-nut
  Sang, happy as he could be,—
"O I live in the heart of the whole
  round world,
And it all belongs to me!"

BY JAMES WHITCOMB RILEY

Little Balser and the **BIG BEAR**

Here is a "cracking good" story. If the language sometimes seems odd, it's because the story was written in 1900, but the plot has not lost any of its intrigue, and the story is as exciting today as it was when your grandfathers and great grandfathers read it in their childhood.

One day Mrs. Brent
took down the dinner horn
and blew upon it
two strong blasts.
This was a signal
that Little Balser,
who was helping his father
down in the clearing,
should come to the house.
Balser was glad enough
to drop his hoe
and to run home.

When he reached the house,
his mother said,
"Balser, go up to the drift
and catch a mess of fish
for dinner.
Your father
is tired of deer meat
three times a day,
and I know
he would like a nice dish
of fried redeyes at noon."

"All right, Mother," said Balser.
And he immediately took down
his fishing pole and line
and got the spade to dig bait.

When he had collected
a small gourdful of angleworms,
his mother called to him,
"You had better take a gun.
You may meet a bear;
your father loaded the gun
this morning,
and you must be careful
in handling it."
Balser took the gun,
which was a heavy rifle
considerably longer than himself,
and started up the river
toward the drift,
about a quarter of a mile away.

There had been rain
during the night,
and the ground near the drift
was soft.

*Little Balser noticed fresh bear tracks, and his
breath began to come quickly.*

Here, Little Balser noticed
fresh bear tracks,
and his breath
began to come quickly.
You may be sure
he peered closely
into every dark thicket
and looked
behind all the large trees
    and logs
and had his eyes wide open
lest perchance
"Mr. Bear" should step out
and surprise him
with an affectionate hug,
and thereby put an end
to Little Balser forever.

So he walked on cautiously
and, if the truth must be told,
somewhat tremblingly,
until he reached the drift.

Balser was but a little fellow,
yet the stern necessities
of a settler's life
had compelled his father
to teach him the use of a gun;
and although Balser
had never killed a bear,
he had shot several deer,
and upon one occasion
had killed a wildcat,
"almost as big as a cow,"
he said.

I have no doubt
the wildcat seemed
"almost as big as a cow"
to Balser when he killed it,
for it must
have frightened him greatly,
as wildcats were
sometimes dangerous animals
for children to encounter.

Although Balser
had never met a bear
face to face and alone,
yet he felt,
and many a time had said,
that there wasn't a bear
in the world
big enough to frighten him,
if he but had his gun.

He had often imagined
and minutely detailed
to his parents and little brother
just what he would do
if he should meet a bear.
He would wait calmly and quietly
until his bearship should come
within a few yards of him,
and then
he would slowly lift his gun.
Bang!
and Mr. Bear would be dead
with a bullet in his heart.

But when he saw
the fresh bear tracks,
and began to realize
that he would probably
have an opportunity
to put his theories
about bear killing
into practice,
he began to wonder if, after all,
he would become frightened
and miss his aim.

Then he thought
of how the bear, in that case,
would be calm and deliberate
and would put *his* theories
into practice
by walking very politely up to him
and making
a very satisfactory dinner
of a certain boy
whom he could name.
But as he walked on
and no bear appeared,
his courage grew stronger
as the prospect
of meeting the enemy
grew less,
and he again began
saying to himself
that no bear could frighten him,
because he had his gun
and he could and would kill it.

So Balser reached the drift;
and having looked
carefully about him,
leaned his gun against a tree,
unwound his fishing line
from the pole,
and walked out to the end of a log
which extended into the river
some twenty or thirty feet.

Here he threw in his line
and soon was so busily engaged
drawing out sunfish and redeyes,

Imagine his consternation when he saw upon the bank,
quietly watching him, a huge black bear.

and now and then a bass
which was hungry enough
to bite at a worm,
that all thought of the bear
went out of his mind.

After he had caught enough fish
for a sumptuous dinner,
he bethought him of going home,
and as he turned
toward the shore,
imagine, if you can,
his consternation
when he saw upon the bank,
quietly watching him,
a huge black bear.

If the wildcat had seemed
as large as a cow to Balser,
of what size do you suppose
that bear appeared?
A cow!

An elephant, surely,
was small compared
with the huge black fellow
standing upon the bank.

It is true Balser
had never seen an elephant,
but his father had,
and so had his friend Tom Fox,
who lived down the river;
and they all agreed
that an elephant
was "purt nigh as big
as all outdoors."

The bear had a peculiar,
determined expression about him
that seemed to say:
"That boy can't get away;
he's out on the log
where the water is deep,
and if he jumps into the river,

I can easily jump in after him
and catch him
before he can swim
a dozen strokes.
He'll *have* to come off the log
in a short time,
and then
I'll proceed to devour him."

About the same train
of thought
had also been rapidly passing
through Balser's mind.
His gun was on the bank
where he had left it,
and in order to reach it,
he would have to pass the bear.
He dared not jump
into the water,
for any attempt to escape
on his part
would bring the bear upon him
instantly.
He was very much frightened
but, after all,
was a cool-headed little fellow
for his age;
so he concluded
that he would not press matters,
as the bear did not seem inclined
to do so,
but so long as the bear
remained watching him
on the bank,

*The bear had a peculiar, determined
expression about him.*

he would stay upon the log
where he was
and allow the enemy
to eye him
to his heart's content.

There they stood,
the boy and the bear,
each eyeing the other
as though they were
the best of friends
and would like to eat each other,
which, in fact,
was literally true.

Time sped very slowly
for one of them,
you may be sure;
and it seemed to Balser
that he had been standing
almost an age
in the middle of Blue River
on that wretched shaking log

when he heard
his mother's dinner horn,
reminding him
that it was time to go home.

Balser quite agreed
with his mother,
and gladly would he have gone,
I need not tell you;
but there stood the bear,
patient, determined, and fierce;
and Little Balser soon
was convinced in his own mind
that his time had come to die.

He hoped that when his father
should go home to dinner
and find him still absent,
he would come up the river
in search of him
and frighten away the bear.
Hardly had this hope sprung up
in his mind,
when it seemed
that the same thought
had also occurred to the bear,
for he began to move
down toward the shore end
of the log
upon which Balser was standing.

Slowly came the bear
until he reached the end
of the log,
which for a moment

he examined suspiciously,
and then, to Balser's great alarm,
cautiously stepped out upon it
and began to walk toward him.

Balser thought
of the folks at home
and, above all,
of his baby sister;
and when he felt
that he should never see them
again,
and that they would
in all probability
never know of his fate,
he began to grow heavy-hearted
and was almost paralyzed
with fear.

On came the bear,
putting one great paw
in front of the other
and watching Balser intently
with his little black eyes.
His tongue hung out,
and his great red mouth
was open to its widest,
showing
the sharp, long, glittering teeth
that would soon be feasting
on a first-class boy dinner.

When the bear
got within a few feet
of Balser—

When the bear got within a few feet of Balser . . . the boy grew desperate with fear and struck at the bear with the only weapon he had—his string of fish.

so close he could almost feel
the animal's hot breath
as it slowly approached—
the boy grew desperate
with fear
and struck at the bear
with the only weapon he had—
his string of fish.

Now, bears love fish
and blackberries
above all other food;
so when Balser's string of fish
struck the bear in the mouth,
he grabbed at them,
and in doing so,
lost his foothold
on the slippery log
and fell into the water
with a great splash and plunge.

This was Balser's chance for life,
so he flung the fish to the bear
and ran for the bank
with a speed
worthy of the cause.

When he reached the bank,
his self-confidence returned,
and he remembered all the things
he had said he would do
if he should meet a bear.

The bear had caught the fish,
and again had climbed
upon the log,
where he was deliberately
devouring them.

This was Little Balser's chance
for death—to the bear.
Quickly snatching up the gun,

he rested it in the fork
of a small tree nearby,
took deliberate aim
at the bear,
which was not five yards away,
and shot him through the heart.
The bear dropped into the water
dead
and floated downstream
a little way,
where he lodged at a ripple
a short distance below.
Balser,
after he had killed the bear,
became more frightened
than he had been
at any time
during the adventure
and ran home screaming.

That afternoon
his father went to the scene
of battle
and took the bear
out of the water.
It was very fat and large
and weighed,
so Mr. Brent said,
over six hundred pounds.

Balser was firmly of the opinion
that he himself
was also very fat and large
and weighed at least as much
as the bear.

He was certainly entitled
to feel "big";
for he had got himself
out of an ugly scrape
in a brave, manly,
and cool-headed manner
and had achieved a victory
of which a man
might have been proud.

The news of Balser's adventure
soon spread among the neighbors,
and he became quite a hero;
for the bear he had killed
was one of the largest
that had ever been seen
in that neighborhood,
and, besides the gallons
of rich bear oil it yielded,
there were three
or four hundred pounds
of bear meat;
and no other food
is more strengthening
for winter diet.

There was also
the soft, furry skin,
which Balser's mother tanned
and with it made a coverlid
for Balser's bed,
under which he
and his little brother
lay many a cold night, cozy
and "snug as a bug in a rug."

An excerpt from *The Bears of Blue River* by Charles Major with drawings by E. J. Baker

A painting for storytelling
by Rosalie Seidler

Meeting

As I went home on the old wood road,
    With my basket and lesson book,
A deer came out of the tall trees
    And down to drink at the brook.

Twilight was all about us,
    Twilight and tree on tree;
I looked straight into its great, strange eyes,
    And the deer looked back at me.

Beautiful, brown, and unafraid,
    Those eyes returned my stare;
And something with neither sound nor name
    Passed between us there.

Something I shall not forget—
    Something still, and shy, and wise—
In the dimness of the woods
    From a pair of gold-flecked eyes.

BY RACHEL FIELD

ILLUSTRATIONS BY CHET RENESON

CHORAL READING

APPEAR
APPEAR
APPEAR
APPEAR
APPEAR

Noodles: Hey, Bill Martin!
They're here, they're there, here they are!
Just like I said they would be.

Bill: Who's here, Noodles?

Noodles: All the boys and girls, can't you see them?
I invited them to help us,
just like I said I would.

Bill: Oh, hello, boys and girls.
Welcome to our party.

Noodles: And say, kids,
you better smile or you won't get any dessert.
I betcha never did know that, did you?
The bigger you smile, the more pie you get.

Bill: This isn't that kind of a party, Noodles.
We're going to do some choral reading.

218

Noodles: Nothin' to eat?
Oh me, I think I have to leave now.

Bill: Wait a minute, Noodles.
We'll have a choral reading party this time,
but the next time
you boys and girls get together
to read your favorite poems and stories,
why not make a party out of it,
with treats for everybody?

Noodles: Well, if there's treats,
don't forget to invite me, O.K.?
Let's start reading.
Sound your do, do, do . . .
I'm in pretty good voice today.
Did you hear my sweet sounds?

Bill: Well, here's the story, "Tatty Mae and Catty Mae"
which I have scored for choral reading.
Let's all choose parts and have a go at it.
There are solo parts and chorus parts.
Everyone will have something to do.

Noodles: Well, I can tell you something right now, Bill Martin,
I'm going to do a solo part
and be in the chorus.
And since this story is about cats,
I'll probably put in a few meows.

Bill: That's a good idea, Noodles.
Boys and girls, you may want to add
sound effects of your own,
such as the sound of sea gulls, and boat whistles,
and cat calls.
Here we go:

ALL:	Two old cats lived on a houseboat.
BOYS:	One was named Tatty Mae.
GIRLS:	The other was named Catty Mae.

SOLO 1:	Tatty Mae was a good fisherman.
SOLO 2:	Catty Mae was a good fisherman.
ALL:	So they both were good fishermen.

SOLO 3:	Tatty Mae left her fish pole in the middle of the room.
SOLO 4:	Catty Mae left her fish pole in the middle of the room.
ALL:	So they both left their fish poles in the middle of the room.

SOLO 5:	Tatty Mae left her fish net hanging on the doorknob.
SOLO 6:	Catty Mae left her fish net hanging on the doorknob.
ALL:	So they both left their fish nets hanging on the doorknob.

SOLO 7:	Tatty Mae left her fish hooks in the bathtub.
SOLO 8:	Catty Mae left her fish hooks in the bathtub.
ALL:	So they both left their fish hooks in the bathtub.

SOLO 9:	Tatty Mae left her fish worms on the dresser.
SOLO 10:	Catty Mae left her fish worms on the dresser.
ALL:	So they both left their fish worms on the dresser.

SOLO 11:	Tatty Mae left her fishing coat on the chair.
SOLO 12:	Catty Mae left her fishing coat on the chair.
ALL:	So they both left their fishing coats on the chair.

SOLO 13:	Tatty Mae put her fishing boots on the bedpost.
SOLO 14:	Catty Mae put her fishing boots on the bedpost.
ALL:	So they both put their fishing boots on the bedpost.

SOLO 15:	Tatty Mae left her fishing cap on the pump handle.
SOLO 16:	Catty Mae left her fishing cap on the pump handle.
ALL:	So they both left their fishing caps on the pump handle.

ALL:	One day Tatty Mae said to Catty Mae,
TATTY MAE:	I declare, you're a litterbug!
ALL:	One day Catty Mae said to Tatty Mae,
CATTY MAE:	I declare, you're a litterbug!
ALL:	So they both said to each other,
TM & CM:	I declare, you're a litterbug!
ALL:	Tatty Mae said,
TATTY MAE:	I think we're both litterbugs!
ALL:	Catty Mae said,
CATTY MAE:	I know we're both litterbugs!
ALL:	So they both said,
TM & CM:	We're both litterbugs!
BOYS:	So Tatty Mae cleaned up and picked up and put away her litter.
GIRLS:	So Catty Mae cleaned up and picked up and put away her litter.
ALL:	So they both cleaned up and picked up and put away their litter.
ALL:	The next day Tatty Mae said,
TATTY MAE:	Where is my fish pole?
ALL:	The next day Catty Mae said,
CATTY MAE:	Where is my fish net?
ALL:	The next day they both said,
TM & CM:	Where are my fish worms?
ALL:	Tatty Mae said,
TATTY MAE:	Now, I'm all mixed up.
ALL:	Catty Mae said,
CATTY MAE:	Yes, the clean-up was a mix-up.
ALL:	So they both said,
TM & CM:	We'll never do it again.
ALL:	And they didn't.

Maybe you'd like to tape record your choral readings.

Conversion

The shrimp said to the lobster,
"Will you spare me?" said the shrimp.

"Why should I spare you?" said the lobster.

"God gave the water for us to swim around in," said the shrimp.

But the lobster whispered,
"God gave me permission to eat shrimps."

"If you were to swallow me
"I would bite your stomach to shreds," said the shrimp.

"I see," said the lobster, and trembled;
"But why didn't the other shrimps bite my stomach to bits?"

"They were cowards," said the shrimp.

From that day the lobster
Became a vegetarian.

A DIALOGUE BY J. T. LILLIE, AGE 10,
COLLAGE BY ERIC CARLE

222

223

When Father Carves the Duck

We all look on with anxious eyes
    When father carves the duck,
And mother almost always sighs
    When father carves the duck;
Then all of us prepare to rise,
And hold our bibs before our eyes,
And be prepared for some surprise,
    When father carves the duck.

He braces up and grabs a fork
    Whene'er he carves a duck,
And won't allow a soul to talk
    Until he's carved the duck.
The fork is jabbed into the sides,
Across the breast the knife he slides,
While every careful person hides
    From flying chips of duck.

The platter's always sure to slip
    When father carves a duck,
And how it makes the dishes skip!
    Potatoes fly amuck!
The squash and cabbage leap in space,
We get some gravy in our face,
And father mutters Hindu grace
    Whene'er he carves a duck.

We then have learned to walk around
    The dining room and pluck
From off the window-sills and walls
    Our share of father's duck.
While father growls and blows and jaws
And swears the knife was full of flaws,
And mother laughs at him because
    He couldn't carve a duck.

BY E.V. WRIGHT

The Railroad Cars Are Coming

The great Pacific railway, For California hail!
Bring on the locomotive, Lay down the iron rail;
Across the rolling prairies
By steam we're bound to go,
The railroad cars are coming, humming
Through New Mexico,
The railroad cars are coming, humming
Through New Mexico.

The little dogs in dog-town
Will wag each little tail;
They'll think that something's coming
A-riding on a rail.
The rattlesnake will show its fangs,
The owl tu-whit, tu-who,
The railroad cars are coming, humming
Through New Mexico,
The railroad cars are coming,
humming
Through
New
Mexico.

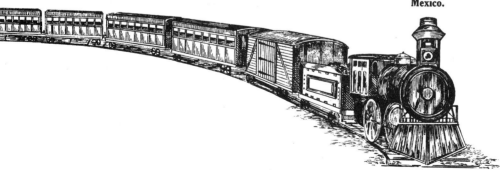

THE RAILROAD CARS ARE COMING
THE RAILROAD CARS ARE COMING
THE RAILROAD CARS ARE COMING
THE RAILROAD CARS ARE COMING
THE RAILROAD CARS ARE COMING
THE RAILROAD CARS ARE COMING
THE RAILROAD CARS ARE COMING
THE RAILROAD CARS ARE COMING
THE RAILROAD CARS ARE COMING

AN AMERICAN FOLK RHYME,
PICTURE BY BETTY FRASER

Gift with the Wrappings Off

All: Oh, what can you do with a Christmas pup
In a little apartment three flights up?
Solo 1: He prowls.

All: And whenever the landlord happens by
With a "Rent's due!" gleam in his fishy eye,
Solo 2: He howls!

All: Or whenever you dress for a hurry date,
With a frantic prayer that you won't be late,
Solo 3: He "helps"!

All: Or when guests sit down in the rocking chair
And neglect to see if a tail is there,
Solo 4: He yelps;

All: And if you protest that he isn't hurt
And call him out from beneath your skirt,
Solo 5: He balks.

All: Or perhaps there's rain, or a two-foot snow,
Or it's three A.M. — then he's got to go
Solo 6: For walks!

All: And the place you pick for his bed at night
Is the one sure place that he doesn't quite
Solo 7: Approve.

All: Oh, what can you do with a Christmas pup
In a little apartment three flights up?
Solo 8: Move?

BY MARY ELIZABETH COUNSELMAN

Jam

"Spread," said Toast to Butter,
  And Butter spread.
"That's better, Butter,"
  Toast said.

"Jam," said Butter to Toast.
"Where are you, Jam,
  When we need you most?"
Jam: "Here I am,

  Strawberry, trickly and sweet.
  How are you, Spoon?"
"I'm helping somebody eat,
  I think, pretty soon."

BY DAVID MC CORD

I'm nobody!

Who are you?
Are you nobody, too?
Then there's a pair of us—don't tell!
They'd banish us, you know.

How dreary to be somebody!
How public, like a frog
To tell your name the livelong day
To an admiring bog!

BY EMILY DICKINSON

BEWARE, or
BE YOURSELF

All: Don't begrudge,
     don't beseech,
     don't besot,
     don't besmirch,
     don't belabor,
     don't belittle,
     don't befuddle,
     don't befog,
     don't benight,
     don't belay,
     don't bedizen,
     don't bedeck,
     don't beguile,
     don't bewitch,
     don't behead,
Teacher: just behave!

BY EVE MERRIAM

The Legend of the Twelve Moons

A CHORAL READING CANTATA

BY RUTH ROBERTS

This is an excerpt from a cantata complete with musical score, available from Michael Brent Publications Inc., 70 Winding Wood Road, Port Chester, New York 10573.

1

The Moon of the Long Snow Falling

1st NARRATOR: It was the last moon of December —
The Moon of the Long Snow Falling.
And the Old Man took the boy by the hand
and began to tell this story:

Many Moons Ago

*Sound Effects:
soft tom toms
gradually getting
louder*

OLD MAN: Many moons long ago
the Indians lived in forest.
They hunted deer, caught fish,
grew corn, trapped beavers;
they had a big sky, laughing streams,
tall junipers, much land,
plenty of buffalo, many moons ago.

1st NARRATOR: And the Old Man drew his shawl up tight,
for the wind of the north blew cold that night,
as he continued his story . . .

228   PASTEL DRAWING BY SHARER

Sharer

229

2

The Moon of the Frost on the Teepee

2nd NARRATOR: It was January—the Moon of the Frost on the Teepee
And the land of the North was sleeping
with snow in the very beginning of time.

BOY: And there were animals . . .

GIRL: Wild animals . . .

BOY AND GIRL: Big . . . gigantic . . . wild . . . animals!

Big Animals

CHORUS: Dum dum dum dum
dum dum dum dum
Over the ice and snow they come
with a dum dum dum dum
Bears so big that
the whole world shook
when they took a single step
and hairy elephants mountain high
with trunks so long they touched the sky
Colossal animals, mammoth animals
dum dum dum dum
Over the ice and snow they come
with a dum dum dum.

*Read with a
steady heavy
rhythm*

BOYS: Then came wandering hunters
with the packs on their backs.

GIRLS: They needed meat so they could eat
and they followed in the tracks of the animals . . .
Big . . . animals . . .

2nd NARRATOR:

And into the strange new land
of the North,
Many hunters came
for many thousand years . . .
And drifted
like flurries of snow in the wind . . .

BOYS:

. . . without any homes
but the shelter of caves . . .

GIRLS:

No worldly goods
but the clothes on their back
And packs of dogs
that followed them.

2nd NARRATOR:

. . . They walked with the sun . . .
and slept with the moon . . .
and their footprints
covered the land . . .

PAINTING BY JESSE WASHINGTON

3

The Moon of the Wolf Grown Hungry

3rd NARRATOR: It was February —
The Moon of the Wolf Grown Hungry —
And now there were tribes who lived in villages
near the Father of the Waters . . .
And they found their food in the sea.
But in winter
only the giant whale could keep them alive
and it had not yet let itself be caught this year.

GIRL: Now Ino and his father
and all the other villagers
were taking their long canoes into the deep icy waters
to let the whale see them and know that they were hungry.

BOY: For Ino, and everyone else, knew
the whale was really a magic man
who had turned himself into a fish
so they would have meat to eat
and oil to rub on their skins.

PAINTING BY CHARLES BREY

3rd NARRATOR: And Ino held tight to the totem pole
on the front of the boat
and shook the magic rattle
to coax the whale out of the water . . .

*Sound Effect:
canoe rippling
through water*

Magic Whale of the Water

INO: Wise whale, pretty whale,
magic whale of the water . . .
Swim a little closer.

CHORUS: Can you hear me, whale?

INO: Swim a little closer
so I can tell you
that I'll dance for you, sing for you,
make feast for you.

*Sound Effects:
ocean waves
and seagulls*

CHORUS: I'll dance for you, sing for you,
make feast for you.

INO: I'll give you pretty feather, whale,
wise whale, pretty whale,
magic whale of the water.

CHORUS: Can you hear me, whale?

INO: Pretty whale, this I tell you,
I'll dance for you, sing for you,
make feast for you.

CHORUS: Oh, I'll show you pretty feathers whale.

INO: Swim a little closer, whale.

CHORUS: Swim a little closer . . .
swim a little closer . . .

3rd NARRATOR: As if by magic,
the giant whale swam closer . . . and closer . . .
and was harpooned and pulled to the beach.
And Ino's promise was kept —
the whale was decorated in splendid feathers
while the villagers danced and sang in his honor.

CHORUS: And when the meat was feasted upon and finished,
each and every bone was thrown back into the water
so the whale could grow together again . . .
and let itself be caught . . .
year . . . after year . . . after year . . .

4

The Moon of the New Spring Waking

4th NARRATOR: It was March —
The Moon of the New Spring Waking —
and among the cliff dwellers of the desert,
Turkey Woman had been blessed with her first grandson.
For many moons she had prepared her home
with dried Indian corn of blue and yellow
and with many painted bowls to make the spirits happy.
Her long hair had been cut with a stone
and woven into tiny stockings . . .
And strands of colored weeds
she had made into a blanket.
But best of all,
she had worked a needle of buffalo bone on white rabbit skin
to make a beautiful pair of tiny moccasins,
for no baby could start on life's journey without them . . .

Two Little New Little Moccasins

TURKEY WOMAN: Two little new little moccasins
for my little papoose to stand straight,
to walk tall, grow to be brave hunter in
two little new little moccasins,
what a journey they'll make.

CHORUS: They'll take him
where the fields are greenest,
where the eagles fly the highest,
where the deer is plentiful
underneath a rainbow sky.

Sound Effects: happy chanting in the distance; a gong sounds to summon the people

TURKEY WOMAN: Two little new little moccasins
tiny white and shiny moccasins . . .
moccasins to wear.

4th NARRATOR: And at midday,
when the sun was brightest,
the women of the village
lowered the long ladders of bark from their cliff houses
and the men climbed up from the fields below
and pulled up their ladders after them
so no enemy could follow.

BOY: And they all stood on the high rocks
and watched Turkey Woman hold up her grandson.

GIRL: So the spirits could see him,
and know him as a child of the cliff dwellers . . .

CHORUS: And many centuries came and passed . . .

DRAWING BY FRANK ALOISE

5

The Moon of the Green Grass Growing

5th NARRATOR: It was April —
The Moon of the Green Grass Growing —
and the giant serpent grew larger every day.

BOY: This pleased the high priests of the temple
as they stood watching,
in copper helmets and silver shirts
that glistened in the sun.

GIRL: For this was not a live serpent,
but a huge mound of earth in the shape of a serpent —
rising high and wide, as far as the eye could see.

5th NARRATOR: And every day the villagers worked with sticks
and clam shells
and animal bones
to move more earth
and make the serpent bigger.
For this was to be their sacred burial ground.

BOY: And as they worked, they sang:

CHORUS: Ay yah!
Ay yah!
(clap, clap)
Ay yah!
Ay yah!
(clap, clap)

*Sound Effects:
chanting, drums,
shells rattling*

5th NARRATOR: . . . And children clapped their hands . . .

And an old man rattled a turtle shell.

*Sound Effect:
shells rattling*

WATER COLOR BY MEL GREIFINGER

5th NARRATOR:	And when the serpent was finished, the tombs were decorated with carvings.	*Sound Effect: blow-pipe music*
GIRLS:	And they held a great feast — for they knew how to store food and preserve it.	
BOYS:	And they danced to the music of the blow pipes they had fashioned from the pieces of copper.	
5th NARRATOR:	Never knowing that the tribe of mound builders would one day vanish with the wind . . .	*Sound Effect: cold wind fades in and out*
	And only the great serpent would remain forever . . .	

6

The Moon of the Woodlands Singing

6th NARRATOR:
It was May —
the Moon of the Woodlands Singing —
and Bright Squirrel was paddling
his birch bark canoe
across the lake
to visit his friend.

*Sound Effects:
birds singing,
water rippling*

BOYS:
And Bright Squirrel's heart
was as happy as the woodlands singing
for he had gathered many berries to bring . . .

GIRLS:
And his mother had sent the sap of a maple tree
which she had made into syrup . . .

SOLO:
And his brother had speared
two rabbits for fresh meat.
This brought Bright Squirrel's friend
much gladness,
for he and his family had traveled
from the White Man's country
far across the great water.
They had landed on the rocky coast.
Now Squanto and Sammoset
and all of Bright Squirrel's people
were helping them —
plant corn . . .
catch turkeys . . .
and learn to live in the Indian country.

6th NARRATOR:	Then at the time of harvest gathering, the Indians made a feast of great Thanksgiving with feelings of friendship for the White Men who had come to their shore.
BOYS:	And they lived in peace ...
GIRLS:	And there was much gladness in the land.

PAINTING BY JACK HEARNE

7

The Moon of the Wild Rose Reddening

7th NARRATOR: It was June —
the Moon of the Wild Rose Reddening —
and the whole village was welcoming
the return of Wise Owl.
For Wise Owl had set forth
on a journey in land
where many new tribes of White Men
had built trading posts.

WISE OWL: The White Men ride on big dogs . . .
They hunt with magic sticks that go BOOM!
They give us great treasure
for our beaver skins.

7th NARRATOR: And the Indians
worked for a whole year
gathering beaver skins.

CHORUS: And they traded the beaver skins
to the White Man
for rainbow trinkets
and ribbons and bows.

7th NARRATOR: And everyone jingled their fine shiny bells . . .
BOYS: put on their beads . . .
GIRLS: and looked in their looking glasses.

7th NARRATOR: And everybody was happy
for there were beautiful beads to wear.

8

The Moon of the Thunder Rumbling

8th NARRATOR: It was July —
the Moon of the Thunder Rumbling —
and a new sound came to the forest.
From high on the hillside,
Little Dipper could see them—
many men swinging giant hammers
over their heads.
They were planting two rows of iron rails
that glistened in the sun . . .

LITTLE DIPPER: Each day as Little Dipper watched,
the men cut down more trees
and planted more iron rails.
And each night
they gathered around a roaring campfire
making loud noises and singing songs.

The Ohio Line

BOYS: Weeds in the summer, briars in the fall
Worms on the watermelon vine
I can't get a girl, so I got none at all
I'm workin' on the Ohio Line

CHORUS: Oh, the Ohio Line
The Ohio Line
Work all day on the Ohio Line
We lay the track
and get an achin' back
On the O-O-O-Ohio Line

242   WATER COLOR BY MEL GREIFINGER

8th NARRATOR: The iron rails grew longer and longer
until they stretched all the way through
the forest.

CHORUS: Then one day a giant monster came . . .
Riding on top of the iron rails . . .
blowing smoke and making thunder . . .
whistling like the wind!
As it came closer and closer
the earth trembled . . .
and the sky shook . . .

*Sound Effect:
train far away
comes closer,
passes
and fades into
distance*

LITTLE DIPPER: . . . and Little Dipper knew
the friendly forest would never be the same . . .

CHORUS: . . . and his family must find a new home . . .

9

The Moon of the Seed Pods Ripening

9th NARRATOR: It was August —
the Moon of the Seed Pods Ripening —
and each new year the giant covered wagons
were rolling further and further west.

TWO GIRLS: Moonflower and her mother
waited until dark
to fill their water jars at the spring.

ALL GIRLS: They feared meeting the White Men
who were ruining the hunting grounds.

BOYS: And in loud voices were ordering the Indians off their land.

9th NARRATOR: The Indians were angry.
The white men were taking their land.
With quick repeating rifles,
they were killing all the buffalo
and driving their spirit underground.

GREY DOVE: And the Elders held council
and began training young braves
in the art of war.

GIRLS: And Moonflower's brother, Grey Dove,
was one of them . . .

9th NARRATOR: And when Grey Dove was ready,
he appeared before the Council of Elders
to give proof of his manhood . . .

BOY 1: . . . the skin of a mountain lion he had killed with his hands . . .

BOY 2: . . . the tail of a rabbit he had shot with his rifle . . .

BOY 3: . . . the stone of a river he had crossed in the current . . .

9th NARRATOR: And the Medicine Man gave him a magic pipe
to bring him much good medicine.
And his father drew his picture in a box of sand,
that the Great Spirit might see him
and give his blessing.

TWO GIRLS: . . . And his mother and his sister, Moonflower,
began sewing bright feathers on a band of weasel skin. . . .

GREY DOVE: For Grey Dove was a warrior now . . .
and would soon wear his first war bonnet . . .

10

The Moon of the Harvest Gathering

10th NARRATOR: It was September —
the Moon of the Harvest Gathering —
and the seeds of hate
had grown for many years.

Sound Effect:
war drums

Angry tom-toms echoed from village to village . . .

Many Moons Ago

CHORUS: Many moons long ago
the Indians lived in forest and hunted deer,
caught fish,
grew corn,
trapped beavers;
they had a big sky,
laughing streams,
tall juniper trees,
much land, plenty of buffalo,
many moons ago.

10th NARRATOR: . . . and the tom-toms reached the Chickasaw,
the Arapaho, the Choctaw . . . Pawnee . . .
Shawnee . . . Cheyenne . . . Sioux . . .

CHORUS: And the tom-toms reached the Blackfoot,
Hunkpapas, Ogalalas . . . Brulés . . .
Apache . . . Comanche . . . Creek . . .

BOYS: The white men made promises,
talked peace, but they spoke "with forked tongues."

10th NARRATOR: . . . And the great war chief councilled
and put on eagle feathers
and led their warriors on the warpath.

CHORUS: ...Sitting Bull...Red Cloud...
Crazy Horse...Cochise...

10th NARRATOR: But civilization had come to the land,
and it was there to stay.

BOYS: ...The end had come to the long ago days...

GIRLS: ...And the Indian had to learn new ways...

CHORUS: ...and make way for the white man.

11th NARRATOR: It was October —
The Moon of the Ravaging West Wind —
and the cavalry was marching...
marching against the last Indian chief to surrender —
the wildest, angriest Indian of them all!
GERONIMO!!!

*Sound Effect:
Indians on
warpath, gradually
fades out*

CHORUS: GERRRRRRRRRRRRRRRRRonimo!!!
GERRRRRRRRRRRRRRRRRonimo!!!

11th NARRATOR: The Apaches came at the sound of his name.
The old, the young, the hunter and warrior
came to follow Geronimo!

BOYS: And they ravaged the earth like the west wind —

CHORUS: ...burning wagons

BOYS: ...raiding the settlers

CHORUS: ...plundering their villages

248

DESIGN BY BERNARD MARTIN

11
The Moon of the Ravaging West Wind

11th NARRATOR:
The U.S. Cavalry men
followed their trail
shouting their boasts:

Geronimo Eats Cactus

BOYS:

Oh, Geronimo eats cactus
Geronimo eats clay
rusty nails and coyote tails,
and rattlesnakes all day.
Geronimo eats vultures,
Geronimo eats bees,
but he could never be
as rough and tough
as the U.S. Cavalry!
(boom! boom!)

*Sound Effects:
the whistling and
marching of the
Cavalrymen
accompanies the
song, sung to
the tune of
"Yellow Rose of
Texas"*

by Ruth Roberts and William Katz

BOYS:	And each Indian fought for *his* sky ...
GIRLS:	*His* streams ...
CHORUS:	His junipers ...
11th NARRATOR:	Fought for *his* land ... fought cold, fought hunger ... until he could fight no more ...
BOYS:	But finally —
CHORUS:	Geronimo had enough.
11th NARRATOR:	He and his people were left with the bitter end of war ...
CHORUS:	... killed ... captured ... or fugitives in hiding.

*Sound Effect:
a cold wind
rises and
gradually fades
out*

12

The Moon of the Tired Hunter

12th NARRATOR:	It was November — the Moon of the Tired Hunter — and Brave Eagle had been fleeing through the woods and mountains for many days and nights.
BOYS:	His horse was gone . . . his rifle empty . . .
GIRLS:	he was cold . . . hungry . . . afraid . . .
12th NARRATOR:	*His* land was now the white man's land,
BOY:	He lived on a government reservation . . .
GIRL:	He was given white man's food . . .
BOY:	White man's clothing . . .
GIRL:	White man's blankets and shelter . . .
12th NARRATOR:	But he kept his own dreams . . .
BOYS:	Kept them alive through the ages . . .
GIRLS:	Kept them alive as his fortress . . .
12th NARRATOR:	Kept them alive generation to generation . . . Kept them alive to be sung today . . . Sung by the Indians proud of their heritage . . .

In Beauty Have I Walked

CHORUS: In beauty have I walked.
All day long have I walked.
All life long have I walked.
Through the returning seasons have I walked.
On the trail marked with sorrow have I walked.
On the trail marked with gladness have I walked.
In young age wandering on a trail of beauty,
      lively, have I walked.
In old age wandering on a trail of beauty,
      lively, have I walked.
In every age wandering on a trail of beauty,
      living again, may I walk.
It will be finished in beauty
    as it was begun in beauty.

HALLOWEEN STORY

AN OLD STORY, DESIGNED BY RAY BARBER

There was an old lady who lived all alone in the woods,
and she wanted someone to come and visit her,
and while she waited she spun cloth:

And still she sat *(fold hands)*
and still she spun *(roll hands)*
and still she waited for someone to come.

Then one dark, dark night
when the old lady was sitting and spinning,
she heard a sound at the door,
and she said, "Come in."
Then SQUEAK went the door,
and in came two big shoes
and sat themselves down
and she thought,

"Oh, how strange to see those big, big shoes

(On that cold cold floor.")

But still she sat *(fold hands)*
and still she spun *(roll hands)*
and still she waited for someone to come.

Soon she heard another sound,
and she said, "Come in."
Then SQUEAK went the door,
and in came two short, short legs
and sat themselves down on the big, big shoes
and she thought,

"Oh, how strange to see those short, short legs

In those big, big shoes

(On that cold cold floor.")

But still she sat *(fold hands)*
and still she spun *(roll hands)*
and still she waited for someone to come.

Soon she heard another sound,
and she said, "Come in."
Then SQUEAK went the door,
and in came a wee, wee waist
and sat on those short, short legs
and she thought,

"Oh, how strange to see the wee, wee waist

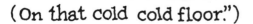

On those short, short legs

In those big, big shoes

(On that cold cold floor.")

But still she sat *(fold hands)*
and still she spun *(roll hands)*
and still she waited for someone to come.

And while she was looking,
she heard another knock at the door,
and she said, "Come in."
Then SQUEAK went the door,
and in flew two broad, broad shoulders
and sat themselves down on the wee, wee waist
and the old woman thought,

"Oh, how strange to see those broad, broad shoulders

On the wee, wee waist

On those short, short legs

In those big, big shoes

(On that cold cold floor.")

But still she sat (fold hands)
and still she spun (roll hands)
and still she waited for someone to come.

And as she was spinning,
she heard another sound at the door,
so she said, "Come in."
Then SQUEAK went the door,
and in jumped two long, long arms
and hung themselves onto the broad, broad shoulders
and the old woman thought,

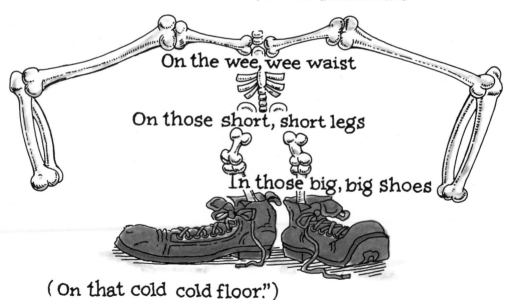

"Oh, how strange to see those long, long arms
On those broad, broad shoulders

On the wee, wee waist

On those short, short legs

In those big, big shoes

(On that cold cold floor.")

But still she sat *(fold hands)*
and still she spun *(roll hands)*
and still she waited for someone to come.

And in just a few minutes,
she heard another sound at the door,
so she said, "Come in."
Then SQUEAK went the door,
and in came two fat, fat hands
and fastened themselves onto those long, long arms
so she thought,

"Oh how strange to see those fat, fat hands
On those long, long arms
On those broad, broad shoulders

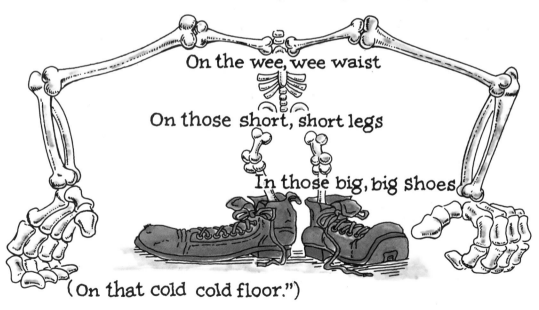

On the wee, wee waist

On those short, short legs

In those big, big shoes

(On that cold cold floor.")

But still she sat *(fold hands)*
and still she spun *(roll hands)*
and still she waited for someone to come.

And then the old woman was beginning to be a little afraid,
but when she heard another sound she said, "Come in."
Then SQUEAK went the door,
and in rolled a round, round head
and sat itself down on those broad, broad shoulders
and she thought,

"Oh, how strange to see that round, round head
And the fat, fat hands
On those long, long arms
On those broad, broad shoulders

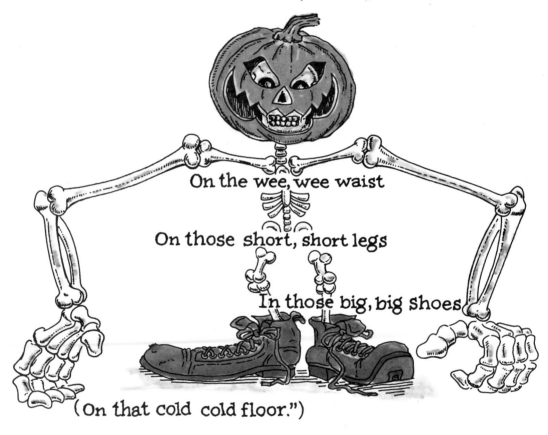

On the wee, wee waist

On those short, short legs

In those big, big shoes

(On that cold cold floor.")

But still she sat (fold hands)
and still she spun (roll hands)
and still she waited for someone to come.

And she said, "Where did you get such big, big feet?"
              "Much walking, much walking."
And she asked, "Where did you get such short, short legs?"
              "Much running, much running."
And she asked, "Where did you get such broad, broad shoulders?"
              "Swinging an axe, swinging an axe."
And she asked, "Where did you get such fat, fat hands?"
              "Threshing wheat, threshing wheat."
And she said, "Well, where did you get such a round, round head?"
              "A pumpkin shell, a pumpkin shell."
Then she asked, "Well, what did you come for?"

This rollicking old ballad has delighted young people generation after generation. It's fun to chant as a choral reading and also to sing as a song. Keep the rhythm at a slow galloping pace with heavy accents. In no time at all, you will have learned it "by heart," and you'll find yourself singing and saying it for a lifetime.

A BALLAD OF A FOX

Solo 1: The fox went out on a winter's night,
And he prayed for the moon to give him light,
For he'd many a mile to go that night
Before he'd reach the town O,
All: Town O, town O,
He'd many a mile to go that night
Before he'd reach the town O.

Solo 2: He ran till he came to a farmer's shed
Where the ducks and the geese were all abed,
Said, "A couple of you are gonna be dead
Before I leave this town O,
All: Town O, town O,
A couple of you are gonna be dead
Before I leave this town O."

Solo 3: He seized a gray goose by the neck,
He laid a duck across his back;
He didn't mind their quack, quack, quack
And their legs all dangling down O,

All: Down O, down O,
He didn't mind their quack, quack, quack
And their legs all dangling down O.

Solo 4: Then old Mother Slipper Slapper jump'd out of bed,
And out of the window she cock'd her head,
Crying "John, John, the goose is gone,
And the fox is over the down O,

All: Down O, down O,
John, John, the goose is gone,
And the fox is over the down O."

Solo 5: Then John ran up to the top of the hill
Where he blew his horn both loud and shrill;
And said the fox, "Keep playin' until
I can get back to my den O,

All: Den O, den O,"
And said the fox, "Keep playin' until
I can get back to my den O."

Solo 6: At last he came to his cozy den,
And there sat his little ones nine or ten;
They said, "Dad, you should go back again,
'Cause it must be a mighty fine town O,

All: Town O, town O,"
They said, "Dad, you should go back again,
'Cause it must be a mighty fine town O."

Solo 7: Well, the fox and his wife without any strife
　　　　　They cut up the goose with a carving knife,
　　　　　And the two never had such a meal in their life,
　　　　　While the little ones chew'd on the bones O,
All: 　　　　　　　　Bones O, bones O,
　　　　　And the two never had such a meal in their life,
　　　　　While the little ones chew'd on the bones O.

—Anonymous,
pictures by Elaine Bolognese

CREATIVE DRAMATICS

Noodles: Hello, Bill Martin.
I'm all ready.
I brought all the stuff...
the costumes
and two homemade spotlights
and the big old black kettle for the soup.

Bill: Noodles, what are you talking about?

Noodles: We're going to give a show, Bill.
Did you forget all about that?

Bill: What show, Noodles?
Do I know it?

Noodles: Heck, yes!
It's the story you told
us about the old man and the old woman
who had the Lord come for supper.
Don't you remember?
It's on page 204.
I always did like that story
so we're going to make a play out of it.

Bill: That's a good choice, Noodles.
It divides easily into scenes.
The first thing you do in making a play
is to figure out the scenes
and what happens in each scene.

Noodles: The first scene could be the old man and woman
making the soup, couldn't it?
And they'll be talking about the Lord coming to supper.
And maybe they'll be singing my song,
"Soup of the evening, beautiful soup!"

Bill: That's the nice part of making a play, Noodles.
You can have the characters say a lot of things
to round out the story.

Noodles: I'm a very good rounder-outer, Bill.

Bill: Just to get things started,
here are some questions
that might help you work out the first scene:
1) What does the little house look like?
2) What and where are the pieces of furniture?
3) Is it a warm day or a cold day?
4) What can the old man and old woman do and say
    that show how very poor they are?
5) Why do they decide to invite the Lord to supper?
6) How do they send him the invitation?

Noodles: Those things really do make us think, Bill,
and I really am a very good thinker.
When we come to those other scenes,
I'll really have some very good questions.

Bill: So will the boys and girls, Noodles.

Noodles: And the best part
is that we don't have to learn any lines, Bill.
We don't even have to write anything down.
We know how the story goes into scenes
so we can just say whatever comes into our little heads.

265

Bill:
That's right, Noodles.
Knowing what is supposed to happen in a scene
let's you think on your feet.
And if you come upon a good way
to say something, you'll probably say it that way
again and again until it becomes part of the show.

Noodles: Watch me walk like an old man, Bill Martin.
I think I could do that part.

Bill: Wow! Noodles, you're good as the old man.
Now let's see some of the boys and girls try it.

Noodles: All right, kids, all you have to do
is walk and talk old,
and you really use an old creaky voice
for the old man and the old lady.

Bill: The boys and girls can choose the actors they like best.

Noodles: And parts can be passed around
so everybody gets a chance
to be the old man if they want to, O.K.?

Bill: Everybody can be in the show
because we'll add a lot of extra parts.

Noodles: Sure, we'll think of a lot of things.
There can be a lot of travelers
passing by the old man's door...

Bill: And there can be an announcer to introduce the play...

Noodles: Bill, do you think there could be a kitty in this play?

Bill: Yes, I think that old man would have a cat...
and maybe a dog.

Noodles: If I was the kitty cat,
I know I would want to smell the soup
and probably sneak a little bitty bite.

Bill:	And there could be a stage crew to handle the lights and the furniture.
Noodles:	And some kids can make all that scenery.
Bill:	Oh, as the boys and girls practice the play, they'll find more and more ways to let everybody take part.
Noodles:	Here's another great idea. You probably didn't know I had so many good ideas, did you, Bill? The boys and girls can make lists of things for the old man and the old lady to do and for the stranger and the two visitors and the cat and the dog.
Bill:	Thinking it through ahead of time makes it easy for actors to become the characters.
Noodles:	I surely do hope they invite me to the show, Bill. Do you suppose they will?
Bill:	Of course, they will, Noodles. You gave them the idea in the first place.
Noodles:	Good old Noodles! Always right there to think of the good stuff to do. Well, I'll be seeing you.
Bill:	Where are you going, Noodles?
Noodles:	To my house to wash my face and sew up the hole in my hat. I really want to look good when I come to the show. Oodeley, oodeley.

MOON BIRD

Sh-h-h-h!

We're gonna catch
a moon bird.

C'mon, Markie!

I'm comin'. Oh, boy,
we're gonna catch
a moon bird.

Oh boy! Oh boy! We're gonna catch a moon bird.

You are looking at pictures from an animated film called *Moon Bird*. You may have seen this film on television or at your local theater, because it has been shown many, many times all over the world. In 1960 when it was made, *Moon Bird* won top awards in the United States and Europe, including Hollywood's Oscar. The creators of *Moon Bird* are John and Faith Hubley. They made the film with the help of their two boys, Mark and Hampy, ages 3 and 6.

Excerpts from a film
by John and Faith Hubley

269

Mr. and Mrs. Hubley told Mark and Hampy what the story was about. Then the boys acted out the story, using their own words, and doing the things that you see in the pictures. What they said was taken down on a tape recorder and later used in the film.

I wanna dig.

You can't, Markie.
You're too little.

But I wanna dig.

Sh-h-h-h!

WAAAA!

Keep quiet, Markie.
You'll scare the
moon bird
away.

Waaaa!

All right, dig.
But keep quiet.

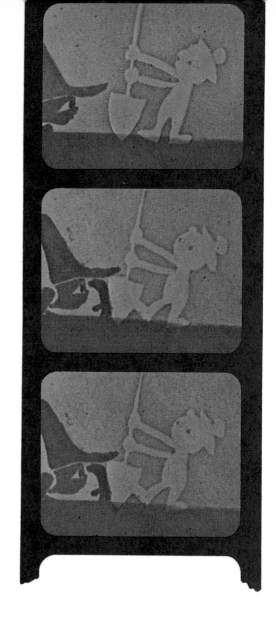

The language we have printed along with the pictures suggests what Mark and Hampy say in the sound film. Mark's voice was used for the character of Markie, and Hampy was his older brother.

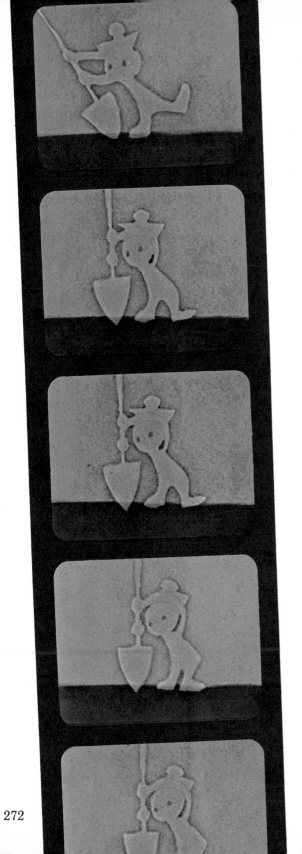

Here, Markie.
You hold the
bait. I'll dig.

Oh, it's candy! Oh, boy!

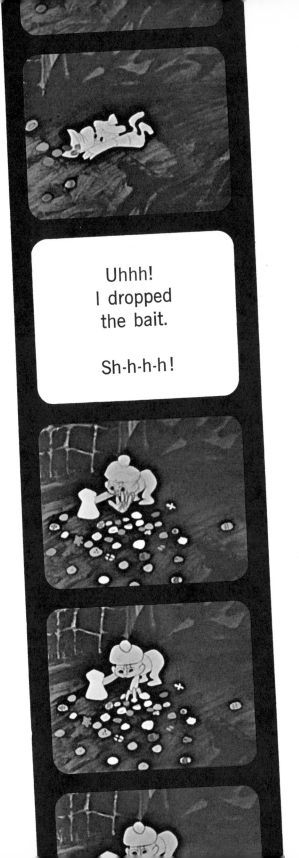

Uhhh!
I dropped
the bait.

Sh-h-h-h!

More than 10,000 drawings were
needed to make the 20-minute film.
Can you figure about how many
drawings were needed for each minute of film?

Hey, you're a
good digger!
Look how deep
the hole is.

Sh-h-h-h-! Markie.

Now I'll set
the cage to
catch the
moon bird.
Sh-h-h-h!

The *Moon Bird* pictures shown here can only suggest what the film is really like. It would be interesting for you to rent a copy of the *Moon Bird* film and compare the show with the story here. What are the advantages of the film and of the book in telling this story?

Oh boy! Oh boy!
Oh, boy!

Let's catch him,
Markie!
Catch him.

Don't run away,
Moon Bird.
Please don't run
away.

Come home with us.
Please.

Please.

Please.

By studying these pictures, can you make up a longer story of *Moon Bird*? It would be interesting to compare your story with the story that the film tells. Who knows, someday you may be making animated films, too!

Here is a delightful song, from the musical play "You're a Good Man, Charlie Brown," sung by the comic-strip characters Charlie Brown (noted in italics as C. B.) and Snoopy.

SUPPERTIME

SONG BY CLARK GESNER   PICTURES BY CHARLES SCHULZ

CB: Hey, Snoopy, are you asleep or something?
I've been standing here with your supper for a whole minute
and you haven't noticed—It's Suppertime—

Snoopy: Suppertime! Suppertime!

Behold the brimming bowl of meat and meal
which is brought forth to ease our hunger.
Behold the flowing flag on moist and sweet
which has been sent to slack our thirst.

CB: Okay, there's no need for a big production.
Just get down off that doghouse and eat—
Oh, Suppertime, Yes, it's Suppertime.
Oh, it's Sup sup suppertime,
very best time of day.
(doo doo doo doo de doo-doo doo)

Suppertime, Oh, it's Suppertime,
And when Suppertime comes can supper be far away.

Bring on the soup dish, bring on the cup,
bring on the bacon and fill me up,
'Cause it's Supper, supper, supper, Suppertime.

CB: Hey, Snoopy, are you asleep or something?
I've been standing here with your supper for a whole minute
and you haven't noticed—

Snoopy: It's Suppertime Suppertime! Suppertime!

Behold the brimming bowl of meat and meal
which is brought forth to ease our hunger.
Behold the flowing flag on moist and sweet
which has been sent to slack our thirst.

CB: Okay, there's no need for a big production,
Just get down off that doghouse and eat—

Oh, Suppertime, Yes, it's Suppertime.
Oh, it's Sup sup suppertime,
very best time of day.

(doo doo doo doo de doo-doo doo)

Suppertime, Oh, it's Suppertime,
And when Suppertime comes can supper be far away.

Bring on the dog food, bring on the bone,
bring on the barrel and roll me home,
'Cause it's Supper, supper, supper, Suppertime.
Suppertime, supper, supper, supper,
Supper, super pepper upper supper,
Super dupper supper time.
Wintertime's nice with the ice and snow,
Summertime's nice with a place to go,
Bedtime, overtime, halftime, too,
But they just can't hold a candle to my Suppertime,
Oh, yeah!

Bring on the hamburg, bring on the bun,
pappy's little puppy loves ev'ry one,
'Cause it's Supper, Supper, supper, supper,
Supper, Super pepper upper,
Supper, Super duper dupper
dup-a- dup-a dup-a-dup-a- dup-a dup-a dup-a dup-a

CB: Now, wait a minute, Snoopy.
(spoken) Hey, get down, you're spilling it all over!
Now cut that out!

Why can't you eat your meal quietly and calmly
like any other dog?

Snoopy: So, what's wrong with making mealtime a joyous occasion?
(very softly) doo doo doo doo-de doo doo doo.

How the
Little Old Woman
Got Her Feather Bed

A story by Hope Newell,
pictures by Ed Renfro

The Little Old Woman had only one blanket for her bed.
It was a nice red flannel blanket, but it was full of holes.
"I must get a new blanket before winter comes," she said.
"Or better yet, I might buy me a feather bed.
How warm and cozy I would be in a feather bed
on cold winter nights!"

But feather beds cost a lot of money,
so the Little Old Woman bought a flock of geese instead.
As she was driving them home from the market,
she said to herself:
"These twelve geese will lay eggs for me all summer.
Then when winter comes, I will pluck their feathers
and make myself a feather bed.
What a clever Old Woman I am!"
When the Little Old Woman arrived home,
she drove the geese into the yard and closed the gate.
Then she ate her supper and went to bed.
The next morning she heard a great noise in the yard.
When she opened the door,
the geese came running to her.
"Honk, honk!" said the big gander, flapping his wings.
"Honk, honk!" said all the other geese, flapping their wings.
Everywhere she went, the twelve geese followed her,
saying, "Honk, honk!" and flapping their wings.
"Dear me," said the Little Old Woman,
"I do believe they want something to eat.
I must buy them some corn."

So she went to the market
and bought a bag of corn for the geese.
Every morning when she opened the door,
the geese came running to her.
"Honk, honk!" they said, flapping their wings.
Then she remembered to give them some corn.
The geese ate so much corn that pretty soon
the Little Old Woman had to buy another bag of corn.
After a while, that bag was empty, too,
and she had to buy another bag of corn.
"These geese eat a lot of corn," she said,
"but after all, they are growing bigger and bigger.

Their feathers are growing thicker and thicker.
They will make me a fine feather bed when winter comes."
By and by the nights began to grow cold.
The red flannel blanket was so full of holes
that it did not keep the Little Old Woman warm.
She shivered all night long.
"Winter will soon be here," she thought.
"It is high time I plucked the geese and made my feather bed."
The next morning she went out to pluck the geese.
"How warm and contented they look,"
said the Little Old Woman.
"They will be cold if I pluck their feathers.
Maybe if I cut the holes out of the red blanket,
it will be warm enough for me."
But when she fetched her scissors
and cut the holes out of the red blanket,
the holes were still there.
In fact, they were bigger than ever.

"What am I to do?" she thought.
"If I take their feathers, the geese will be cold.
If I do not take their feathers, I will be cold.
I suppose I had better use my head."
And here is how the Little Old Woman used her head.
First she tied a wet towel around her forehead.
Then she sat down with her forefinger against her nose
and shut her eyes.
She used her head and used her head and used her head.
She used her head so long that it began to ache,
but finally she knew what to do.
"The red blanket is no good to me," she said.
"I will cut it into twelve pieces
and make each of the geese a warm red coat.
Then I can pluck their feathers to make me a feather bed."
The Little Old Woman set to work
and made each of the geese a little red coat.
On each coat she sewed three shiny brass buttons.
"Now I must pluck the geese and make my feather bed,"
said the Little Old Woman.

She took a basket and went out to pluck the geese.
She plucked the big gander and put his feathers in the basket.
She plucked the gray goose and put her feathers into the basket.
Then she plucked the other geese
and put their feathers into the basket.

When all the geese were plucked,
the Little Old Woman put a little red coat on each goose
and fastened it with the shiny brass buttons.
"How handsome the geese look," she said.
"I was very clever to think of making the little red coats
to keep them warm."
Then she carried the basket of feathers into the house
and sewed them into a strong ticking to make a feather bed.

When the bed was all finished,
the Little Old Woman said to herself:
"I shall sleep very warm this winter.
How wise I was to buy a flock of geese to make a feather bed.
It all comes of using my head."

Noodles: Did you know what I've been doing now, Bill?
I have a new friend and you know what his name is?
His name is Dick.
And we were out hunting for ooley bugs.
Did you know what an ooley bug is?

Bill: I never heard of an ooley bug, Noodles.
What's an ooley bug?

Noodles: Well, I never did really see one but I'm looking,
and you have to wear your hat
when you look for them—that's why I have my hat on—
because you wait until it gets dark
and you go out the front door
and you go into the bushes—

then you keep bending
low to the ground and saying,
"Ooley bug! Ooley bug!"
and if there's one there,
it'll come right up to you.
You never did know this?

Bill: I never knew that, no.

Noodles: I know just about every thing in the world,
and if you just stay with me, Bill Martin,
you'll probably —

Bill: — catch an ooley bug, right?

Noodles: Yes, but if you don't catch one,
I'll put one in my pocket and bring him to you.

Bill: That's an interesting word, Noodles,
ooley bug!

Noodles: I just made it up, Bill.
When I get tired of the old words,
I just make up new ones.
I write them on the wings of paper airplanes
and sail them out into the world for everybody.

Bill: What are some of you home-made words, Noodles?

Noodles: Fingertonguelingersome is one.

Bill: What?

Noodles: Fingertonguelingersome.
And you're supposed to say it very very fast.

Bill: What does it mean?

Noodles: Bill Martin, do you know what?

Bill: What?

ANTIDISESTABLISHMENTARIANISM

Noodles: You sound like a school teacher.
They think you have to know what every word means.
Sometimes you just say a word because it's pretty
or because you like the way it rolls around on your tongue.
Fingertonguelingersome is a loop-de-looper.
It just flies around your mouth
and sometimes it comes out differently
than it's supposed to.

Bill: I'll remember that one, Noodles.

Noodles: And do you see these cards, Bill?
They're my word cards.
I write my special words on cards
and carry them around with my flashlight.
So I can look at them day and night.

Bill: That's an interesting pack of words, Noodles.

Noodles: And that isn't all I do. I write my special special
favorite words on colored paper and paste them
on a great big potatoe chip can,
and use that same can for my waste basket.
Nobody's going to throw
my good words away.

Bill: Where do you find your words, Noodles?

Noodles: Every place.
Sometimes when I hear a word I like,
I just say, "That's my word."
And I take it.
Did you know something, Bill?

Bill: What?

Noodles: Sometimes I hang some words
on a string that goes
from one side of my room to the other.
Right now the words on my string say,
"Chickamungus is amazable."

superfluous

lunar module

powwow

eventide

miracle

Superstar

halo

kingpin

Stupidhead

flashback

rough 'n ready

Bill: Say, that's a good word — *amazable.*

Noodles: I made it up, Bill.
And do you know something else?
I've got my best words
right here on my arm.

Bill: Noodles, you're kidding.

Noodles: Do you want to see?
But first you gotta promise
you won't wash them off.

Bill: I promise.

Noodles: Then take a little look, Bill Martin.

Bill: Wouldn't you know it!
"Oodles of Noodles!"

Noodles: That's the true one.
Do you know where I found these words?

Bill: Where, Noodles?

Noodles: I made them up out of my own little head.
When I was in the Hall of Mirrors once,
I saw myself 53 times all at once.
And I just said,
"There's oodles of that dear sweet little Noodles."
And now I've got to go.

Bill: Where, Noodles?

Noodles: Word hunting.
Goodbye, Bill.
Oodeley, oodeley!

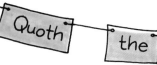 

The Big Red Dragon

story and pictures
by Jay Ells

The little animals lived in a
castle high on a rock
in the sky.
A big red dragon with
three heads protected
the castle.
He loved the little
animals.

By day
he was a thin blue cloud
keeping watch.

At night
he was bats in flight
keeping guard.

In summer
    he was rainstorms
    and lightning
    keeping lookout.
        In winter
            he was snowflakes
            and ice
            keeping vigil.

One evil day a wicked giant
sneaked up on the castle.
He was hungry for little
animals.

The big red dragon became
two charging reindeer
and jumped on the
giant.

The two charging reindeer became seven flying cats and swooped down on him.

The seven flying cats became five hungry alligators that bit and snapped and snarled.

The five hungry alligators
became a family of sharp-
toothed pandas and
chewed and chunked and
chomped.
The family of sharp-toothed
pandas became

303

a thin blue cloud that

ate the giant wherever
it touched him.....
and devoured him.

Now the thin blue cloud
tried to change back into
the big red dragon with
the three heads.
It tried and tried, but its
magic was worn out.
It just broke apart into
wisps and

drifted away.

The little animals flew a red
flag with three tails in
memory of the big red
dragon with the three
heads.
The flag looked a little like
the protector dragon
himself.

Then, lo! One spring evening above the castle a thin blue cloud formed like a halo around a Christmas angel.

It grew and grew.

A rainbow formed around
the thin blue cloud.
The little animals cheered
and cheered.
They knew that the big red
dragon had returned.

Chen Chi 1966

A Vagabond Song

There is something in the autumn that is native to my blood—
Touch of manner, hint of mood;
And my heart is like a rhyme,
With the yellow and the purple and the crimson keeping time.

The scarlet of the maples can shake me like a cry
Of bugles going by.
And my lonely spirit thrills
To see the frosty asters like smoke upon the hills.

There is something in October sets the gypsy blood astir;
We must rise and follow her,
When from every hill of flame
She calls and calls each vagabond by name.

A POEM BY BLISS CARMAN,
PICTURE BY CHEN CHI

GOING BEYOND
R·E·A·D·I·N·G

"I CALL IT RESEARCH."

Bill: Noodles! Noodles!
        I thought he was here.
        I'm sure I heard him. . . .
        Noodles!
        Oh Noodles, where are you?

Noodles: Here I am, Bill.
            Couldn't you see me?

Bill: No. I looked everywhere
        but you weren't to be seen.

Noodles: I didn't want you to find me because
            I was researchin', didn't you know that?

Bill: Researching what?
        I didn't know you even knew what research is.

Noodles: You never do seem to know what I know.
I know a very lot of things if you would only ask me.

Bill: All right, Noodles, tell me about researching.

Noodles: Well, for one thing, Bill,
it's something you do yourself.

Bill: Like what?

Noodles: If you get to wondering about something,
and I do this many times,
you just ask yourself your own questions
and then you find out your own answers.

Bill: Give me an example, okay?

Noodles: Well, the other day I read an article in the paper
about wanting to have school all year long,
and so I just asked myself,
"Who in the world wants school all year long?"

Bill: That's a good research question.
How did you go about it?

Noodles: To start with I went right to the kids and asked them,
because they're the ones who are going to be involved.
I asked ten kids.
I have 8 no's, 1 yes and 1 undecided.
And I'll tell you something else, Bill Martin,
that you probably wouldn't know unless I tell you.
All 8 said it big, loud, and *NO*.

Bill: Did they explain why
they didn't want school all year long?

Noodles: That was my second question
that I asked them, "Why?"
Here's what they said,
I wrote it down:

The first one said,
    "What are you trying to do, kill me?"
The second one said,
    "What! Give up my vacation?"

The third one said, "I'm undecided. It all depends on
    what you're going to do in school those extra months."
The fourth one said, "Oh, my aching head!
    I couldn't stand that much learning!"
The fifth one said, "Why not? School's okay.
    It's better than doing nothing."
The sixth one said, "My mother wouldn't like that. She'd
    have to mow the grass herself if I went to school."
The seventh one said. "Never. What would teachers
    be like if they were stuck with us all year long!"
The eighth one said, "I'd lose my baby-sitting money
    if I went to school and I need my money."
The ninth one said, "What a gyp!
    Just when I'm old enough to go to camp,
    they start talking about school all summer."
The tenth one said, "You must be kidding!"

So there you have my research, Bill Martin.
Eight no's, 1 yes, and 1 undecided.

Bill: That's a good kind of action research, Noodles,
    getting people's opinions and counting them up.
    How did girls feel about this question
    as opposed to the boys?

Noodles: I don't know.
    I didn't ask any girls, but that's a good idea.

Bill: Boys and girls, why don't you do some research
    in your own classroom,
    and ask these same questions of each other
    and tally them as boys' opinions and girls' opinions.
    And see if boys and girls think alike on this question.

Noodles: And another thing, they might find out what the teachers
    in the school think.

Bill: And how about your mothers and your fathers?

Noodles: And if you want the opinion of a ghost,
    just let me know, kids.
    I'll get you a great big fat *NO* vote.

Bill: And there are other kinds of research you might like to do.
For example, if you read a poem that you really like,
you may want to try to find other poems by the same author.
Or poems about the same subject.
And there's action research, such as finding out who broad
jumps the farthest;
opinion research, such as finding out what people believe;
library research, such as reading to find more information;
experiment research, such as finding out whether a plant
grows better indoors or outdoors.

Noodles: And ooley bug research where on some dark and stormy night
you go hide in the bushes calling for ooley bugs
to come out of their little holes and be counted.

Bill: Or if you read about a place and get curious about it,
you may want to look at a map and find out where it is,
or you might want to call a travel agent
for a brochure about that place.

Noodles: Or if you're a ghost and want to go visit the place
you just say

Goodbye, Bill Martin.
This is too much research for me.
Oodeley, oodeley!

Bill: Noodles! Come back! Come back!
I have a lot more to tell you about research. . . .
Well, boys and girls, I can tell you. . . .
Boys and girls!
Now how could they do that?
They've disappeared too.

A story by Hertha Pauli

Letters by Frank Aloise

A VOTE FOR A BEARD

Abraham Lincoln

Grace sat in her little room, writing a letter by the light of an oil lamp. It was very late. In the upper right-hand corner of the page, she wrote her address and the date:

Westfield, Chautauque Co NY
Oct 15, 1860

When her father wrote to important people, he always addressed them by their last names with "Hon." and two initials in front. Now how was she to address Mr. Lincoln? Grace knew that "Hon." meant honorable. Surely Mr. Lincoln was honorable. But what were his initials? She knew only his name, Abraham. People called him Abe. "Old Abe," or "Honest Abe." So Grace made a quick decision and wrote:

Hon A B Lincoln
Dear Sir
My father has just come from the fair and brought home your picture and Mr. Hamlin's.

No, that wouldn't do. First of all, she would tell him who she was.

I am a little girl only eleven years old but want you should be President of the United States very much so I hope you wont think me very bold to write such a great man as you are.

In black and white her boldness made her uneasy again. Would he even answer a letter from a little girl? He must have a lot to do right now, getting people to vote for him. And there surely would be many letters from grownups for him to read and to answer. She wrote:

Have you any little girls about as large as I am if so give them my love and tell them to write to me if you cannot answer this letter.

She stopped again. She would have to get to the point soon, or he would not even finish reading her letter and would never know her good advice.

I have got 4 brothers.

But two of them, she thought, don't have any whiskers, and then suddenly she knew, and from now on the writing went fast, without much worry about punctuation; the safest way was to leave out anything you didn't know.

. . . and part of them will vote for you any way and if you will let your whiskers grow I will try and get the rest of them to vote for you you would look a great deal better for your face is so thin.

All the ladies like whiskers and they would tease their husbands to vote for you and then you would be President. My father is going to vote for you and if I was a man I would vote for you to but I will try and get everyone to vote for you that I can.

Grace paused for breath. She felt much better now, having told him everything that was important. She held the picture of Abraham Lincoln up to the light. The hollows were back in the cheeks. But she did not want to make him feel bad about the picture.

I think that rail fence around your picture makes it look very pretty...

I have got a baby sister she is nine weeks old and is just as cunning as can be.

What was that? Was someone coming up the stairs? She had to finish in a hurry. She didn't want anyone to know she was writing a letter to Mr. Lincoln. She scribbled on hastily, misspelling a word and crossing it out again; even the grammar got all tangled up. But there was no time to rewrite the letter now.

*When you ~~direct~~ your letter direct to
Grace Bedell Westfield
Chautauque County New York*

Yes, someone was coming!

*I must not write any more
answer this letter right off
Good bye   Grace Bedell*

There was no time to read over what she had written. She folded the letter into an envelope, addressed it, and sealed it with wax. Now, if only Mr. Lincoln will answer my letter Grace thought. But when his reply actually came, she was nonetheless amazed.

*Miss Grace Bedell
Westfield, Chautauque County
New York*

U.S. POSTAGE
THREE CENTS

Private

Springfield, Ill.

Oct. 19, 1860

Miss Grace Bedell

My Dear little Miss,

    Your very agreeable letter of the 15th
is received. I regret the necessity of saying
I have no daughters. I have three sons,
one seventeen, one nine, and one seven
years of age. They, with their mother, con-
stitute my whole family. As to the whiskers,
having never worn any, do you not think
people would call it a piece of silly affection
if I were to begin it now?

    Your very sincere well-wisher,

    A. Lincoln

But the greatest surprise of all was yet to come.

Grace was overwhelmed to learn that Abraham Lincoln, the President-elect, would pass through her town on his way to Washington to be inaugurated President of the United States.

When the day came, Mr. Lincoln's inaugural train pulled into Westfield where hundreds of people had gathered to greet him. Grace, hanging onto her father's hand, strained to see the man whom she had written to several months ago.

Suddenly, there he was, a tall, lean man with a black hat, walking out onto the platform of the train. Abraham Lincoln. Grace couldn't take her eyes from his face. He *was* wearing a beard, and he looked just as strong and handsome as she imagined he would look.

"Ladies and gentlemen," he said, "I have no speech and no time to speak in. I appear before you today that I can see you and that you may see me." His voice was clear and he held the crowd. "As I am en route to Washington to be inaugurated your President, I have but one question to ask. These are difficult times and I will need your help. Will you stand by me, through the difficult times ahead, just as you now are standing with me?"

Historical events often tell a story such as this. The happenings in this story are true, but they are as exciting as any created by a writer of fiction.

At first no one spoke, not a murmur. Then, from out of the crowd, a voice rose up: "We sure will, Abe! We'll stand by you!"

Everyone became excited and began to shout and cheer. "Yes—yes—we sure will, Abe! We will all stand by you!"

Slowly the shouting died and Abraham Lincoln went on: "I have a little correspondent in this place," he said, "a little lady who wrote me a letter."

Grace's heart suddenly began to pound. She clutched her father's hand tighter.

"This little lady saw from the first what great improvement might be made in my appearance," he said, "... and if she is present, I would like to speak to her. Is Grace Bedell here?"

Grace wasn't sure what happened next because she was so excited, but she found herself being led forward through the crowd toward the train platform where Abraham Lincoln was standing.

And now her father was boosting her up to the platform in sight of everyone she knew in Westfield, and, before she knew it, she was standing beside Mr. Lincoln.

The President-elect stooped, raised Grace high in the air, kissed her on both cheeks, and gently set her down again.

"You see, Grace, I let my whiskers grow as you asked me to. Do you like them?"

"Oh, yes, Mr. Lincoln," she said shyly.

Mr. Lincoln smiled, "Thank you, Grace," he said, and he lifted her down from the train into her father's hands. It was February 16, 1861, a day Grace Bedell would never forget.

Of all the hunting animals
that roam the woods,
the cleverest is the red fox.
One of the most amazing signs
of his cleverness
is the fact
that he can live and grow fat
within the limits of towns
and even big cities.
I was driving into Kansas City
along U.S. Highway 50
one morning
during the rush hour
when I first spotted *my* fox.

He was a magnificent dog-fox,
standing on an embankment
watching the cars whiz by.
He stood firmly on his black legs,
ears pointed,
sniffing the air.
The wind rippled
his red coat
and his long, silver-tipped tail.
Every time thereafter
that I drove by the place
where I had first seen my fox,
I looked carefully for him.

RED
FOX

An essay by Bernard Martin,
with pictures by William Reusswig

And my efforts were rewarded.
I saw him again several times.

The fact
that the fox was growing fat
within the city limits
was proof of his cleverness
and hunting skill.

Unafraid of the stream
of noisy, speeding traffic,
he had invaded the city limits
in search of food
and, perhaps, a mate.

The cunning of foxes
allows them to survive
in unbelievable numbers
in the midst of men and dogs
and modern developments.
It is said that
throughout the United States,
there is one fox
for every fifty acres
of farmland.
I live in Missouri
and know plenty of places
where I can stand,
either in the early morning
or evening hours,
to see a fox pass.

The fox
is one of woodland's happiest
and most expert hunters.
He enjoys the chase,
delights in play,
and thoroughly loves the hunt.
Although he eats everything
from fruit to birds,
he is especially good
at catching rats.
Few animals
can match his hunting skill.
His training as a hunter begins
when he is five weeks old.
At that time,
usually late April,
he comes out of the den
in the earth
where he was born.
With his brothers and sisters,[1]
he spends the first two months
of his outdoor life
near the entrance of the den,
chasing leaves and butterflies
and pouncing on weeds
that wave in the breeze.

[1]sometimes called *litter-mates*

His parents teach him
the skills of hunting
by bringing home
small live rodents[2]
so that he can practice
catching them.
The parent foxes
carry the rodents home
held tightly but unharmed
in their mouths.
They free the small animals
in front of the fox pups
and, instinctively,
the pups spring after the rodents.
In a short time,
the fox pups become expert
at pouncing on their prey.

At the beginning of winter,
each of the young foxes
is ready to leave home
and "go it on his own."

A fox leads an orderly life.
He hunts on regular trails
that wind and crisscross
through the woods
and over the fields.
These trails have been made
by the fox himself
as he makes regular rounds
through his hunting grounds
looking for food and play.

I often come upon such trails
as I wander
across the countryside.
A fox lays claim to the trails
in his territory
by leaving his droppings[3]
as markers.
Each big rock and log
along the trail
is also marked
with the scent of his urine
to tell other foxes,
"No Trespassing."

One fall day
as I was standing in a thicket,
I saw a fox
use his great hunting skills
just for the sport of it.
As he loped along the path
on that frosty morning,
he skidded to a stop.
His nose had told him
that a mouse was nearby.

He whirled suddenly
and pounced on a log
that lay a dozen feet
off the trail.
In a matter of seconds,
he dug a fat field mouse
out of a hole
in that rotten log.

[2]rats, mice, gophers, chipmunks, *et cetera*   [3]his excretions

Then the fox's fun began.
He let the mouse go, unharmed,
in the center
of a small clearing.
When the mouse tried to escape,
the fox pounced on it
with perfect aim
and gently brought it back
to the center of the clearing
to be released again.

This went on
for at least fifteen minutes
before the fox lost interest.
Then he killed the mouse
and buried it in a hole
that he dug near the log.

Before trotting happily
on his way,
he sprayed the spot with urine
so that later,
when he was hungry,
he could return to the spot,
guided by his nose,
and dig up a meal.

During the spring
the fox is a most serious hunter.
He has to be, for it is then
he has several mouths to feed.
His mate, called a *vixen*,
has whelped a litter
of one to twelve pups.
The pups[4] are always hungry
and devour everything
that the parents capture.
The parent foxes need
all the stealth
and cunning and speed
that nature has given them
to provide
for their hungry,
yapping young.

When the pups are older,
the fox family
goes hunting together.
A red fox family
on a single hunt
may catch eight pounds or more
of rodents, rabbits and chickens.

[4]also called *kits*

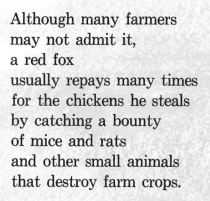

Although many farmers
may not admit it,
a red fox
usually repays many times
for the chickens he steals
by catching a bounty
of mice and rats
and other small animals
that destroy farm crops.

Last spring, a big red fox
came into a field where I stood.
He stole softly along,
raising wet nostrils
above the tall weeds
to test the air.
All of a sudden,
he seemed to turn
into a bouncing, golden-red ball.
A frightened mouse
fled through the thick weeds,
and the fox jumped high
to catch sight of it.

After half a dozen high leaps,
the chase ended
as quickly as it had started.
The master hunter trotted off,
carrying the squirming mouse
back to his hungry family.
Or was he, perhaps,
taking it back to his den
to teach his youngsters
how to hunt?

The Cornfield

I went across the pasture lot
When not a one was watching me.
Away beyond the cattle barns
I climbed a little crooked tree.

And I could look down on the field
And see the corn and how it grows
Across the world and up and down
In very straight and even rows.

And far away and far away —
I wonder if the farmer man
Knows all about the corn and how
It comes together like a fan.

A POEM BY ELIZABETH MADOX ROBERTS,
PICTURE BY MICHAEL LOWENBEIN

MAKING JUDGMENTS

Noodles: Say, Bill, like I told you,
my very favorite story is "Cracker and Fletcher."

Bill: Why, Noodles, just last week you told me
that your favorite story was "Freddy Freon."

Noodles: That's one of my problems.
I'm always changing my favorite.

Bill: Join the crowd, Noodles.
That's the problem everyone has.
Our favorite story generally
is the one we just finished reading.

Noodles: Sometimes that's true but sometimes
my favorite is something that I read a long time ago.

Bill: That's the way we come to make judgments
about our likes and dislikes, Noodles.
Sometimes a favorite story may lose its first place
the very next day,
while another favorite story
may stay on the list for years and years.

340

Noodles: What list, Bill?

Bill: Your hit parade of favorite stories.

Noodles: And favorite poems and pictures.

Bill: That's right, Noodles.

Noodles: And favorite books and teachers
and specially our favorite days.

Bill: Noodles, let's make a preference line
of your favorite stories.

Noodles: A what line?

Bill: A preference line.
That's a way of deciding
what stories you like best.

Noodles: Oh, I already decided that, Bill.
"The Three Billy Goats Gruff"
is my favorite story of stories.

Bill: Then let's put that story at
the high end of your preference line.

The Three Billy-Goats Gruff

LOW   MIDDLE   HIGH

Noodles: Can I put my awful story at the low end?
It's that story called "The Twins Visit the Farm."
It wasn't much of a story.
It was just a lot of dry facts
that somebody thought we should learn.
And that dumb Susie!
I was really disgusted with her.
Facts, facts, facts.

Bill: All right, we'll put "The Twins Visit the Farm"
at the low end of your preference line.

Noodles: And I know another dumb one that goes at the low end,
"Mat Has A Fat Bat."
That's a fake story.
Just a bunch of words!

Bill: Noodles, you're sounding like my puppet.
Could it be that I'm putting words in your mouth?

Noodles: I don't need your words, Bill.
I've got plenty of my own.

Bill: Good for you, Noodles.
Now let's put "Fat Mat Cat" on the line.
Where do you want it?
Near the middle or near the bottom or at the bottom?

Noodles: Do you have a basement for such stuff?
It was the worst I've ever read,
so extend that low line, Bill.
Let's make room for one that is lower than the low.

Bill: Okay, Noodles, we'll put it here.

Noodles: Those two low ones are crowding each other
out of the picture.

Bill: And your favorites will crowd each other,
too, for the top slot, Noodles.
Choices are not easily made.

Noodles: Well, I'd rather move to the top.
It was sure crumby at the bottom.

Bill: But, Noodles, knowing what you don't like,
helps you know what you do like.
Every preference line has to have a bottom.

Noodles: Even for desserts.
I put all those delicious desserts at the top.

Bill: Oh no you don't Noodles.
Some people call stewed prunes dessert.

Noodles: They do?
And I don't even like the way they smell!

Bill: Boys and girls, now that you've seen
how a preference line works,
why don't you make a preference line of your own —
one for stories, another for poems,
another for songs, and so forth?
Every story that you read will fit
somewhere on the line.
A story may change places
from day to day or week to week,
but it can always be represented
after you've read it.

Noodles: That would really take a long line, Bill Martin,
longer that I have time to fill in,
so I've got an idea.
I'm only going to put ten stories on my line,
ten stories I've read this last month.

Bill: Well, you can do it anyway you please, Noodles,
and now before you beat me to it,
oodeley, oodeley!

DISAPPEAR
DISAPPEAR
DISAPPEAR
DISAPPEAR
DISAPPEAR

Noodles: Do you believe that?
Ol' Bill Martin just did my disappearing act.
Just wait till tomorrow,
I'm really going to trick him.
I'm going to get him good.

TRULY THE LIGHT IS SWEET AND A PLEASANT
THING IT IS FOR THE EYES TO BEHOLD *the sun.*

—Ecclesiastes

Photographed by HIRO

"Well, so long. See you next September."

Facts About Angry Bears

An angry bear can rip a man
to shreds in a matter of minutes.
Anyone who has encountered
a king grizzly in battle
and lived to tell the tale
is a lucky person indeed.
Although a bear looks large
and awkward,
it is surprisingly fast.
When it attacks, it "explodes."
A man's best defense
against a dangerous bear
is his rifle.

A bear usually gives a warning
of its anger.
A low moaning sound
rising to an awesome roar
is often a bear's way
of announcing its attack,
but sometimes its noise
is a bluff.
If a bear can scare a man away
and steal his food
without a fight,
particularly if the man has
some freshly killed meat
that the bear desires,
why fight?
But if the bear moves in
to give battle,

it "buttons its ears back"
against its head
and comes roaring into a charge.
Its eyes burn green.
Foam bubbles from its open jaws,
and it covers the ground
with incredible speed.

A bear is a massive[1] animal.
It slashes both with its sharp claws
and with its fangs,
moving faster than any man
can move.
It can grab a man in its teeth
and shake him like a rag doll,
much like a vicious[2] dog
might battle a chicken.
A man's only defense
at a time like this
is to play dead
in hope that the bear
considers the battle finished
and goes away.

Bears, like people,
vary greatly in temperament,[3]
but all bears seem to be curious
about people.
They often will watch a man
as if they wanted to understand
what he is "all about."

[1]huge   [2]mean   [3]disposition

Illustration by Robert Kuhn

Sometimes a fisherman
in bear country may discover
that a bear or several bears
have been following him
for a long time,
watching him fish.

Young bears seem unafraid
of men,
but they don't have much time
to become friendly
because their mothers
send them running to safety
whenever a man appears.
If a mother bear thinks
that her cubs are in danger
of an approaching man,
she prepares for a fight.
There is nothing
much more dangerous
than a mother bear
protecting her young.
Another bear that is dangerous
is one that once was wounded
or shot at by a man.
That bear carries a grudge,
and he generally attacks
any man he sees,
whether or not the man
is threatening him.
A vicious bear
sometimes gives no warning
of his attack.
The first warning a man gets
is the sight of the bear
sailing toward him.
Despite their enormous size,
bears can move silently
through the forest brush
in preparing to attack.

Through the ages,
bears have been kings of the woods.
No animal could outfight them—
until man developed a rifle.
Bears now sense
that man is dangerous,
but they in no way admit
that man is their master.
Even though a man carries a gun,
bears are unafraid.

In the short period of 75 years,
bears have been so hunted
and preyed upon by man,
that they are fast disappearing
from the earth.
They survive today
in only a few protected places.
The cutting of forests
as man has taken
more and more land
for homesites and farming
has crowded bears
into smaller and smaller areas.
Bears that once ruled the forests
now have almost no place left
where they can find enough food
to maintain themselves.
Crowded together as they are
in small regions,
they rapidly are losing their battle
with man and his ways.

History of the Hot Dog

Frankfurter,
wiener,
wienie
or hot dog—
whatever you call it,
it is still
one of America's favorite foods.
Billions of them are eaten
by Americans every year.
If all the hot dogs
eaten by Americans in 1966
were tied end to end,
the string would be
762,000 miles long—
a distance equal
to 32 times around the world
or one and a half round trips
to the moon.

The hot dog is as American
as apple pie or ice cream.
The hot dog, however,
did not originate in this country.

The hot dog is really
a kind of sausage.
Sausages were eaten
3,500 years ago
by the Babylonians
and also by the ancient Greeks
and Romans.
The hot dog
as we know it today
did not come into existence
until about 1852
when a butcher in Germany
made a sausage with a "new look."

It was long and round.
He called his new sausage
a *frankfurter*,
taking the name
from the city of Frankfurt
where he lived.

At about the same time
a similar kind of sausage
was becoming popular in Austria.
This new sausage was associated
with the capital city
of Vienna (or Wien,
as the Austrians spell it),
and so it became known
as a *wiener*.
When the frankfurter, or wiener,
was introduced to America,
it became known
by yet another name.

It was often called
a *dachshund sausage*
because of its
peculiar resemblance
to the long, thin dog
of that name.
But by any name,
it was popular food,
especially at carnivals,
circuses, theaters
and fairs.
It did not get its final
and most colorful name,
however,
until it was first served
at a ball game
in the year 1900.

The game was being played
at the New York Polo Grounds.
The weather was cold.
The food vendors knew
that ice cream and soda pop
were not appropriate,
so they featured
hot dachshund sausages,
kept warm in small tanks
of boiling water.
"Hot dachshund sausages!"
they cried.
"Get your hot dachshunds here!"
The chilled ball fans
ate the steaming sausages
and called for more.

A fan watching that game
was the famous cartoonist
Tad Dorgan.

He had been drawing
a series of cartoons
about a talking sausage,
but as yet
he had not given
the sausage character a name.
As he heard the cries
of the vendors,
"Get your hot dachshunds here,"
he decided to call
his talking sausage
the "Hot Dachshund."
But, like a lot of other people,
Tad Dorgan was uncertain
about how to spell *dachshund*,[1]
so he simply called
his sausage cartoon character
Hot Dog.

[1]Like the sausage itself, the
word *dachshund* also comes
from Germany. It means
badger hound.

Or would you
rather eat
a hamburger?

That's how the hot dog
got its name.

When hot sausages
were first served
at the New York ball park,
they were lifted directly
from the boiling water
and eaten without a bun.
Customers kept switching them
from hand to hand
to keep the hot sausages
from burning their fingers.

Then, in 1904,
at the St. Louis World's Fair,
a German sausage vendor
named Antoine Feuchtwanger
began to wrap
his sizzling hot dogs
in bread rolls.
These rolls
not only kept the customers
from burning their fingers,
they improved the taste,
especially when the hot dogs
were drenched with mustard,
catsup, relish or sauerkraut.
The fame
of Feuchtwanger's hot dog
spread so rapidly
that the hot dog
served in a roll or bun
became one of America's
favorite foods.

The taste and food value
of a hot dog
depend on its ingredients.
The favorite hot dog
contains about 60 per cent beef
and 40 per cent pork.
This combination of ground meats
is blended with salt and spices
and stuffed into a skin.
There are hot dogs, however,
that are made entirely of beef,
and still others
that have no meat in them at all.
The hot dogs eaten by vegetarians
are made entirely of vegetables
which have been spiced
and wrapped in such a way
that their taste and appearance
are very similar to that
of a beef and pork hot dog.
The latest hot dog
to be tried on the public
is made out of chicken meat.
What is it called?
A *bird dog*, of course!

VIEWING THE PRINTED PAGE AS ART

Noodles: Say, Bill,
you're giving me
a headache.
You've got me hanging here upside down.

Bill: Sometimes a page in a book
needs a special touch to make it come alive, Noodles.

Noodles: Why did you do it to me?
Just let the old words do it.
They don't care if they're upside down.

Bill: We've done that, too, Noodles.
Sometimes the words in this book have run crossways,
sometimes downwards,
sometimes upwards,
sometimes round and round.

Noodles: And sometimes there aren't any words at all.

Bill: The important thing is that the page.
gives the reader a deep sense of aliveness.

Noodles: That's what I like, Bill Martin.

Bill: Sometimes the words alone possess the aliveness,
sometimes it's the combination of words and pictures,
and sometimes it's just pictures.

Noodles: And sometimes it's Noodles.
Don't forget me, Bill.

Bill: That's right, Noodles.
You've given many of these pages
a keen sense of aliveness.

Noodles: Well, I think I'll go now.

Bill: Not yet, Noodles. I'm not finished.

Noodles: I'll help you finish Bill.
Don't look now but I'm going to turn you
into a blot.

Bill: Not again, Noodles, please.

Noodles: We need some aliveness on this page.
I think you'll look better as a blot.

Bill: Please, Noodles, I'm not finished.

Noodles: Here comes the big surprise:
Hokus pokus diddeley dokus
presto chango — Bill Martin is a blot!

As you go through this book, boys and girls,

Well, what do you know!
Nothing stops him.
Talk, talk, talk, talk, talk.
I think I'm going home
to get my earmuffs.

ask yourself what makes a page come alive for you.

Goodbye, everybody.
Oodeley, oodeley!

Sometimes it's the words, sometimes the white space, someti.....

my little brother A PICTURE FOR FAMILY REMEMBRANCES

If once you have slept on an island

You'll never be quite the same;
You may look as you looked the day before
    And go by the same old name.

You may bustle about in street and shop;
    You may sit at home and sew.
But you'll see blue water and wheeling gulls
    Wherever your feet may go.

You may chat to the neighbors of this and that
    And close to your fire keep,
But you'll hear ship whistle and lighthouse bell
    And tides beat through your sleep.

Oh, you won't know why, and you can't say how
    Such change upon you came,
But—once you have slept on an island
    You'll never be quite the same!

A POEM BY RACHEL FIELD,
PICTURE BY TED RAND

THE FLAG GOES BY

Hats off!
Along the street there comes
A blare of bugles, a ruffle of drums,
A flash of color beneath the sky:
Hats off!
The flag is passing by!

A POEM BY HENRY **HOLCOMB** BENNETT
PAINTING BY ALLAN MARDON

You're a Grand Old Flag

You're a grand old flag,
You're a high flying flag;
And forever, in peace,
May you wave;
You're the emblem of
The land I love,
The home of the free and the brave.
Ev'ry heart beats true, under Red, White and Blue;
Where there's never a boast or brag;
But, should auld acquaintance be forgot,
Keep your eye on the grand old flag.

A song by George M. Cohan

Here Is This Night

What though the day
be filled with weariness,
with many a jarring sound
and fretful sight,
here is this night.

Whatever went before,
here is an hour
of clear pure dark
with peace on wood and hill,
and every quiet pool
brimful of starlight,
and the wind's all still.

The day went hard
and with tomorrow's light
will come new care.
But here is a space
of dusk and dew and dreams.
Here is this night.

BY NANCY BYRD TURNER

City Lights

Into the endless dark
The lights of the buildings shine,
Row upon twinkling row,
Line upon glistening line.
Up and up they mount
Till the tallest seems to be
The topmost taper set
On a towering Christmas tree.

BY RACHEL FIELD

PHOTOGRAPH BY ARTHUR SELLER

African Dance

A poem by Langston Hughes

The low beating
of the tom-toms,
The slow beating
of the tom-toms,
Low . . . slow
Slow . . . low–
Stirs your blood.

Dance!
A night-veiled girl
Whirls softly into a
Circle of light.
Whirls softly . . . slowly,
Like a wisp of smoke
around the fire–
And the tom-toms beat,
And the tom-toms beat
And the low beating
of the tom-toms
Stirs your blood.

Dance the Boatman

All: The boatman he can dance and sing
And he's the lad for any old thing.

Boys: Dance the boatman, dance!
Dance the boatman, dance!

Girls: He'll dance all night on his toes so light
And go down to his boat in the morning.

All: Hooraw the boatman, ho!
Spends his money when he goes ashore!
Hooraw the boatman, ho!
Rolling down the O-hi-o!

AN ANONYMOUS CHANTY

Old Man Rain

All: Old Man Rain at the windowpane
Knocks and fumbles and knocks again;
His long-nailed fingers slip and strain:

Girls: Old Man Rain at the windowpane.

Boys: Old Man Rain.

All: Old Man Rain at the windowpane
Reels and shambles along the lane;
His old gray whiskers drip and drain:

Girls: Old Man Rain with fuddled brain
Reels and staggers like one insane.

Boys: Old Man Rain.

Girls: Old Man Rain is back again,
With old Mis' Wind at the windowpane
Dancing there with her tattered train:

Boys: Her old shawl flaps as she whirls again
In the wild-man dance and is torn in twain.

All: Old Mis' Wind and Old Man Rain.

BY MADISON CAWEIN

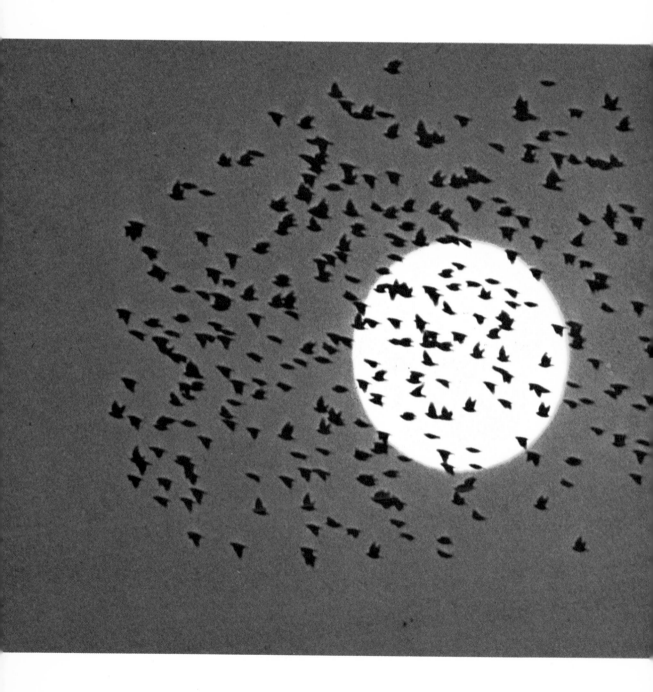

This poem is a picture, and the picture is a poem. This is the way with art. It helps you become aware of new relationships.

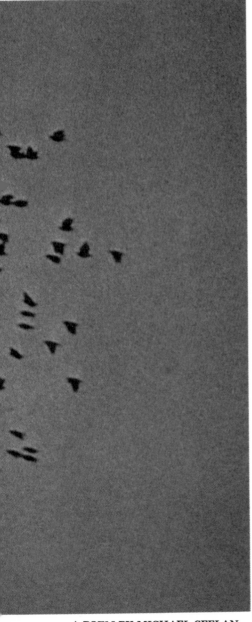

Swifts

I saw them twist and dart and turn,
And then I saw them dive and wheel,
In the sky and in the breeze
And round the trees and back again.

I saw them sweeping to the clouds,
And shaking off the pattering rain,
Beaks to the sunset every one,
Wings for the morning, day was done.

I saw them hover, hold, and glide,
A tiny, lovely cavalcade
Of lovers of the sun and rain,
Waking so they could sleep again.

A POEM BY MICHAEL GEELAN,
PHOTOGRAPH BY HIRO

There's the kind of walk you walk
When the world's undone you,
There's the kind of walk you walk
When you're walking proud,
There's the kind of walk you walk
When the neighbors shun you,
There's the kind of walk you walk
Sets you 'bove the crowd,
There's the kind of walk you walk
When somebody loves you
When you feel as if you're walking on a cloud.

Good fortune found you chappie,
And your life's a happy valentine
When you're Walking Happy
Don't the bloomin' world seem fine?

There's the kind of walk you walk
  When you feel like crowing,
There's the kind of walk you walk
  When you're on your way,
There's the kind of walk you walk
  When your pride is showing,
There's the kind of walk you walk
  When today's your day,
There's the kind of walk you walk
  When the world's all rainbows
And your heart is hoppin' like a popinjay.

So you best believe it chappie,
Your life is finger snappy
The day you learn that Walking Happy
Gives the world a shine.
  So just keep Walking Happy
With your hand in mine.

Walking Happy

A song by Sammy Cahn,
pictures by Tom O'Sullivan

Primer Lesson

Look out how you use proud words.
When you let proud words go, it is not easy to call them back.
They wear long boots, hard boots; they walk off proud; they can't
    hear you calling—
Look out how you use proud words.

BY CARL SANDBURG

A Painting for Poetry

by N. Calabrese

Sissa and the Troublesome Trifles

NOW IT HAPPENED in the old days that King Balahait[1] was ruler of a province in India. One day he called for his adviser, Sissa.[2]

"Sissa," the king shouted angrily, "it is not possible for a king to do everything himself. He must have advisers to do his work."

"That is true, O Greatest of Kings," Sissa said mildly.

"My other advisers take care of important problems for me," the king went on, his temper growing hotter. "Why don't you do the same?"

"O King, live a thousand years," Sissa said. "I work hard."

"O King, live *two* thousand years," spoke up Rhadama,[3] another of the king's advisers and a man most jealous of Sissa. "Surely Sissa works *hard*, but he never does anything when he works!"

[1] pronounced Bah-lah-HAIT
[2] pronounced SIS-sə
[3] pronounced Hrə-DAH-mə

"O King, live *three* thousand years," said Devatta,[4] still another adviser. "Yesterday I inspected the army for you. Rhadama counted your treasure. Indra collected your taxes. But when Sissa was supposed to repair your garden, he wasted his time listening to the complaint of an old beggar woman!"

"O King, live *four* thousand years!" spoke up Indra. "The day before yesterday, Sissa wasted time looking for a lost child!"

"O King, live *five* thousand years!" Rhadama said, "Sissa is forever wasting time with trifles such as this when he should be worrying about the king's problems."

The king looked at Sissa. "What should I do with you?" he asked, his voice heavy with rage.

"O King, live *six* thousand years," Sissa said. "I do not know what you should do with me."

"What should I do with him?" the king asked the others.

They hesitated. Although they hated Sissa themselves, they knew that the king loved the old man for all his faults. They were afraid to seem too harsh.

[4] pronounced Day-VAH-tə

"O King, live *seven* thousand years," Indra began slyly. "Why not give Sissa another chance? Then if he fails this last chance, he must be banished."

"That is good advice," the king said. "Rhadama, give Sissa a task to do for me. Let it be something of importance."

"O King, live *eight* thousand years!" the evil adviser said, smothering his glee. "Now it is known that our great king is a lover of peace, but other kings are always fighting him. Let Sissa find a way for all men to live and fight the wars which they must fight without killing anyone!"

"Is that possible?" the king asked. "Oh, I wish it were. I am tired of killings."

"Oh, it must be possible!" the three enemies of Sissa cried together. "We are sure Sissa can do it."

"Fine," the king said. "Sissa, this is your last chance to serve me. Solve this problem, and you shall be my Grand Vizier.[5] Fail and I must banish you forever. Since I cannot permit one to leave who knows the palace secrets, I will have no choice but to chop off your head."

The three evil men smiled, for they thought Sissa would not be able to solve the problem. "O King, live *forever*!" they cried.

"O King, live forever and a day," Sissa said. "I will go to the mountains and return in a month with the solution."

"O King, live forever and *two* days—" Indra said. "I——"

"Oh, be quiet!" the king snapped. "I am sick of this live so long business. Rest assured I will live as long as I can. And I don't think your silly wishes will help me at all. Go, Sissa. I expect you back in one month."

Now within a week the evil men reported to the

[5] pronounced Vih-ZIR;
the highest official

king that their spies claimed that Sissa was not working on the problem at all. Instead the old man was sitting in the shade of a tree, carving little men and animals from ivory while he listened to trifling complaints brought to him by the villagers.

This saddened the king, for he really loved his old adviser. However, he had given a king's word that Sissa would be killed if he failed. This could not be changed although the king regretted now that in his anger he had made the promise.

Finally, it was the end of the month. Sissa came back to court. He brought with him the toys he had carved during his stay in the mountains. Gravely he set a checkered board in front of the ruler. Then he placed the little figures upon it. There were tiny castles, war elephants, grand viziers, soldiers, and two kings and two queens. All together they made two armies. One was white ivory. The other was ivory stained black.

"Lord of all the lands!" Sissa said. "Live as long as you wish. On this board, which I have named the Royal Game of Chess, men can make war against each other without killing. The rules of chess are the same as the rules of war. A leader must play it the same as he would plan his strategy on the battlefield."

"O King!" cried Rhadama. "No game can take the place of real fighting. Sissa is trying to trick us. He has not solved the problem at all. He must be banished.

The king has given his royal word."

"I suppose you are right," the king said thoughtfully, looking at the chessboard with interest. "But I would like to try the game myself."

"O King," Sissa said. "I do hear tell that the King of the South is talking of war against our kingdom. Why not try the game with him?"

The king agreed and sent a challenge to the rival king to meet him on the battlefield of chess.

And it was arranged. The two kings fought across the checkered board for days. They plotted like generals leading armies. They attacked with their foot soldiers. They smashed lines with their elephants. They made sly thrusts with their viziers. And they sent their knights charging against the enemy.

But neither could win. Their great battle was a draw. When the rival king saw how closely each was matched with the other in his knowledge of the arts of war, he decided that it would not be wise to attack King Balahait with a real army. The war was called off.

The king was both amazed and overjoyed. He called his advisers and told them how Sissa's game had indeed permitted them to fight without killing anyone.

Sissa's enemies glowered with rage as the king asked the old man to name his reward.

"Just some rice, O King," Sissa said. "And let it be measured by the chessboard which I have invented. Place one grain of rice on the first of the sixty-four squares of the board. Then place two grains on the second square. Four on the third, doubling each amount until the sixty-four squares are covered."

"Sissa!" the king cried. "How can any man be so wise as to invent chess and so stupid as to ask for such a trifle reward? You have been this way all your life. It was the same when you wasted time from my big problems to listen to the villagers' small ones."

"O King, this is the reward I ask," Sissa said stubbornly.

"Then let it be so," the king said. "I thought you had learned to be wise. I see I was wrong."

Sissa only smiled as the rice was brought. One grain was placed on the first square and swept into a bag for Sissa. Two grains were placed on the second, four on the third, and eight on the fourth. By the time they came to the tenth square, it was necessary to measure out 512 grains. This was doubled to make 1,024 for the eleventh square. By the time they got to the twentieth square, the amount was over a half million grains.

The king looked uneasy and looked searchingly at Sissa who only smiled.

Soon rice filled all the sacks, covered the floor, and ran out the windows.

"How much rice is it going to take to double the amount for sixty-four times?" the alarmed king asked.

"I cannot speak so great a figure," Sissa said, "but I will write it down."

And on the marble wall, he wrote:

"18,466,744,073,709,551,615."

The king gasped. "There isn't that much rice in the world! How can such a little thing add up to so much?"

"It is the same with small troubles, O King," Sissa said gently. "All together they are very large, even though each may be small in itself. Then they are so great that they can crush a kingdom."

"I see," the king said slowly, "I also see now why you spent so much time listening to the small troubles of my people. You have proven to me that I was wrong."

"The king is very wise," Sissa said.

"Now you may ask for another reward for teaching me the value of small things," the king said, "but please, Sissa! Make it a *big* one, for rich as I am, I cannot afford another of your *small* rewards!"

"For my other reward I ask only that this rice be given to the poor of the country," the old man said.

"So let it be," the king said. "And as an additional reward, I appoint you my Grand Vizier to see after all the little problems of the people of my kingdom. You are to see that they do not add up like your doubled grains of rice until they become so big they crush our kingdom."

And it is written that Sissa took the job and did very wisely at it.

An East Indian folktale,
retold by I. G. Edmonds,
pictures by Elaine Bolognese

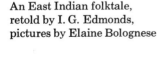

I was directed by my grandfather
To the East,
    so I might have the power of the bear;
To the South,
    so I might have the courage of the eagle;
To the West,
    so I might have the wisdom of the owl;
To the North,
    so I might have the craftiness of the fox;
To the Earth,
    so I might receive her fruit;
To the Sky,
    so I might lead a life of innocence.

A POEM "DIRECTIONS" BY ALONZO LOPEZ

The Writers' Reader HONORS COLLECTION:
1962-1966 INSTITUTE OF AMERICAN INDIAN ARTS
SANTA FE, NEW MEXICO

PAINTING BY YEFFE KIMBALL, HANDLETTERING BY JAY ELLS

Here's a Picture for Pondering

An Action-Sequence Painting by Ray Burdzinski

You'll Never Walk Alone

When you walk through a storm,
Hold your head up high,
And don't be afraid
Of the dark.
At the end of the storm
Is a golden sky,
And the sweet silver song
Of a lark.
Walk on through the wind,
Walk on through the rain,
Though your dreams be tossed and blown.
Walk on, walk on, with hope in your heart,
And you'll never walk alone,
You'll never walk alone!

A song by Richard Rodgers and Oscar Hammerstein II,
picture by Albert John Pucci